WHAT CHURCH LEADERS ARE SAYING
ABOUT *UPSIDE-DOWN KINGDOM* . . .

Pastor Bill White gives us a fresh look and new insights into the words of Jesus known as the Beatitudes. Bill shows us that God's way doesn't always make sense to us. Sometimes the logical and the theo-logical don't add up in our minds. However, in the mind of God, they always lead to a blessed life. Few pastors have what it takes to lead a church in a city as diverse and as unchurched as Miami. Pastor Bill White of Christ Journey is one of those pastors. Under his leadership, Christ Journey has grown into a large and leading Miami church.

Dr. Rick Blackwood
Retired Lead Pastor of Christ Fellowship
Miami, Florida

Bill White is a pastor with vision. Since the day we met in 2007, I've considered him to be a member of our family because of his love for us. His positive attitude and loving nature have come through clearly as he joined us in reaching the Middle East with the love of Christ. His presence at our 20th anniversary celebration in Beirut was encouraging.

Chaouki Boulos
Pastor/Director of Living Faith Ministry International
Beirut, Lebanon

The alignment of Bill White's scholarship, integrity, and unconventional ("Jesus-like") ministry are on full display in *Upside-Down Kingdom*. I've known Bill for years, and the wonderful thing about this book is that Bill lives this stuff.

Dr. Travis Collins
Former missionary and author, Senior Pastor of First Baptist Church
Huntsville, Alabama

I've read the Sermon on the Mount so many times that I can almost recite it by heart, but Bill White gives us a fresh look at the first part of it: the Beatitudes. These nine statements are paradoxical, enigmatic, and odd . . . and at the same time they're beautiful, powerful, and right. If we understand them and incorporate them into our lives, we'll experience more of God's love and strength than ever before. That's what we all need, isn't it?

Sidney Costa
Lead Pastor of Igreja Batista Memorial
Alphaville, São Paulo, Brazil

Pastor Bill White has written a "cutting edge" book on leadership and teamwork! He focuses on the "Be Attitudes"—which are found in the opening lines of the Sermon on the Mount. He describes the relationship between attitudes, actions, and the rewards of blessings. Those who prove to be faithful with their talent on ordinary days will be successful when opportunity comes. They will be rewarded by the success of their daily walk with the LORD, and those who build into the lives of others receive joy in the success of their teammates!

Steve DeBardelaben
Chaplain of the NBA Miami Heat
Miami, Florida

I became a Christian under Pastor Bill's teaching as a teenager in the Miami-Dade County Public School system. Over the last 25 years of my life and my experience on the mission field, my spiritual walk has been profoundly impacted by the depth of Bill's teaching and his genuine relationship with Jesus. Jesus' words in The Sermon on the Mount are deep and profound, and their impact on our lives is not limited by our place in history or the culture where we live. Pastor Bill's insights into the Beatitudes are certain to take you into a deeper relationship with Jesus, no matter who you are or where you live. It is a true blessing to have his teachings in print.

Christopher Farrington, MDiv
Open Hearts International Relief Mission
Nicaragua

In *Upside-Down Kingdom*, Bill White invites us to join him in exploring one of Christ's greatest messages. Not only will you be challenged by the other-worldly dynamics in Jesus' words, but you will also resonate with Bill's fresh insights into the "impractical practical" kingdom life. I found the perspectives luminating, life-giving and rich—unpacking Christ's message in areas of my life where I need it most. Bill has been my pastor, leader, and boss, but more importantly, a friend for many years. I know this book has been a labor of love. When you read it, you'll find out why.

Greg Gackle
Interactive Team Leader and Pastor at Life.Church
Coral Gables, Florida

With piercing insight and practical wisdom, this book unlocks the treasure bound up in the Beatitudes of Jesus. Written from the heart of a pastor, Bill White takes the reader on an adventure into the reality of the kingdom Jesus came to earth to prepare us for!

Cal Jernigan
Lead Pastor of Central Christian Church of Arizona
Phoenix, Arizona

I know of no servant of Jesus that would be more suitable than Dr. Bill White to write a book interpreting the teachings of Jesus in the Beatitudes. Just as Jesus displayed the intuition of God in declaring these culturally radical words, my friend Bill ministers masterfully in the diverse world of Miami, Florida, with the creative intuition of Jesus.

Dr. Ron Lyles
Senior Pastor of South Main Baptist Church
Pasadena, Texas

The primary way that Jesus described His mission to establish the kingdom of God was to preach "the Gospel of the Kingdom." Those of us who love Jesus and long to follow His ways often struggle with finding our role within this Jesus movement. Bill White's *Upside-Down Kingdom* lays out simple, powerful steps that Jesus-followers can take to cooperate with God's Spirit in becoming transformed and joining Jesus on this kingdom adventure. If you long to become more faithful and effective, I challenge you to dive into this book.

Kevin Palau
President and CEO of the Luis Palau Association
Portland, Oregon

This book by Dr. Bill White—my senior pastor, mentor, and a close family friend—is a *unique* focus with an *unfamiliar* perspective on the Beatitudes: instead of looking at them from *our* standpoint, we should understand and apply them from *Jesus'* perspective! Bill's talents of mining and contemporizing God's Word and applying his vast knowledge and practical experience to it as a Minister and Servant of God for more than 45 years, come through vividly in every one of the 30 chapters. With his observational acuity, he offers readers fascinating perspectives to ponder and discuss so they can apply the Beatitudes in their daily lives. *Upside-Down Kingdom* is a wonderful addition to all believers' libraries, written by a man who epitomizes humility, integrity, and passion for the one and only Living and Loving God of our universe!

Dr. David J. Sumanth
Professor Emeritus at the University of Miami; Honorary Exec. Pastor of
Cornerstone Prayer Fellowship Church, Guntur, India; and Co-Founder,
Paul J. Sumanth Ministries, Inc.

We pick up books for different reasons. Today's Christians appear to be losing their relevancy in culture, and as a follower of Christ, I am concerned. Bill's book addresses this cultural angst by wonderfully revisiting the greatest sermon Jesus ever preached. We are reminded, with insights and practical applications, what it is about Jesus and following Him that makes the difference. We are reminded that "it's not about me," and that Jesus' playbook is a lot different than anything we are used to. Are you ready to see things differently and to be radically encouraged? Then start reading *Upside-Down Kingdom*.

Stephan N. Tchividjian
Co-Founder and President of National Christian Foundation
Ft. Lauderdale, Florida

The Sermon on the Mount is one of the most beloved sermons of all time, but ironically, it's also one of the most misunderstood sermons of Jesus. Pastor Bill White shows us that the way to live the blessed life, the right-side-up life, is by following the upside-down teachings of Jesus from this sermon. Pastor Bill walks us through the first part of the Sermon on the Mount the same way he shepherds his church: thoughtfully, honestly and helpfully. Not only is this an excellent treatise on the Beatitudes, reading it warmed my heart. It will warm yours too.

Jim Tomberlin
Pastor, author, and church consultant
Founder of MultiSite Solutions
Colorado Springs, Colorado

Bill White writes as a passionate Christ-follower—contagious in his desire that others find the path to a blessed and purposeful life. He writes as a pastor—wise and sensitive to the honest questions that would-be disciples of Christ ask as they consider the call to follow Jesus, and gifted in his ability to communicate with clear and compelling language. He writes as a student of Scripture—careful and thoughtful in his understanding and interpretation of the biblical text. Bill White is all of these as he guides us in the path of following Christ who gives us the Beatitudes—a call to a right-side up life in an upside-down world. This book is an excellent study for personal reflection, small group study, and for church-wide application for developing mature disciples along the path Jesus himself outlined for us.

Allen Walworth
Executive Vice President of Generis
Atlanta, Georgia

No one promotes the gospel better than Bill White. His book on the Beatitudes is brilliantly written and thoroughly engaging. Whether Bill is telling the story of repelling down a ten-story building to raise money for Youth for Christ or sharing the pathos of leading the funeral service of a dear young mother, this book is a page-turner. Every story will help you navigate through the Beatitudes and experience genuine transformation.

Rich Wilkerson, Sr.
Lead Pastor of Trinity Church
Miami, Florida

Bill White has given us an invaluable look into the heart of Jesus' message conveyed through the Beatitudes. Bill is a pastor first, and so his insights, stories and applications will be especially appreciated by those of us who seek to bring the Good News to people as our vocational calling. As his friend, I know that Bill lives out what he teaches, preaches and asks others to do. He is so right: Jesus wants us to live an upside-down life, and to discover that it is actually right-side up! Thank you, Bill for this guidebook for doing just that.

Dr. Bill Wilson
Director of The Center for Healthy Churches
Clemmons, North Carolina

WHAT MARKETPLACE LEADERS
ARE SAYING ABOUT
UPSIDE-DOWN KINGDOM . . .

This book is an easy-reading, practical guide for spiritual growth. It invites individuals, study groups and churches into an inspirational and profound voyage of reflection, prayer and action. The reading begins with accepting our need for God, and then invites us to become His instrument through His grace. It's a journey worth taking.

Odilon Almeida
Board Director of Millicom International and Former President of
Western Union Global Money Transfer
Coral Gables, Florida

In *Upside-Down Kingdom*, Bill White shares a refreshing look at the Beatitudes, and he shows us that Jesus is the hero of the story. In his unique style of communicating, Bill challenges us to take our spiritual life to the next level, but it's not self-effort—he removes the pressure to perform and replaces it with God's grace, love, peace and joy.

Luis Chiappy
Executive Vice President of AXA Advisors, LLC
Miami, Florida

Pastor Bill White's book, *Upside-Down Kingdom*, is a great addition to your "self-care toolbox." May we access the kingdom by the power of the Holy Spirit. May our affluence look different than the world's affluence. May we choose the ultimate adventure and audacity of living by loving others as Jesus loved us. To God be the glory!

Blanca Correa-Cespedes, EdD
Senior Assistant Principal of Miami Beach High School, wife, mom, and
passionate family advocate
Miami, Florida

Dr. Bill White has written a book that will appeal to biblical scholars and casual readers alike. *Upside-Down Kingdom* is a "deep-dive" into one of the most popular—and yet most misunderstood—parts of the Bible: the Beatitudes. While most people have read the Beatitudes, which are the beginning of the Sermon on the Mount, many do not understand the true meaning of Jesus' message. Dr. White's straightforward but provocative and inspirational analysis of these "blessings" challenges our thinking—and provides us a new perspective of Jesus' love for mankind.

Brian Keeley
President and CEO of Baptist Health South Florida
Coral Gables, Florida

The concepts and principles in this book are easy to understand, yet they are deep and rich with practical applications—it's a great devotional. Pastor Bill unpacks upside-down Beatitudes and applies them to the daily life of a Christian. I have seen him apply these truths in his own leadership and welcome him sharing them with others.

Tova J. Kreps, LCSW
President of Wellspring Counseling
Miami, Florida

If you're looking for a match to ignite your spiritual growth, this is it. In *Upside-Down Kingdom,* Pastor Bill White explains the Beatitudes in a way I've never seen or heard before—a way that's both revolutionary and makes perfect sense. When I read it, I thought, *Why didn't I see this before?* It doesn't matter . . . I see it now.

Arva Moore Parks McCabe
Historian, author, preservationist
Miami, Florida

This book is like finding the "X" on a treasure map! "Dig here to find the mystery of God's treasure for our lives in the profound puzzle of Jesus' teaching on the Sermon on the Mount!" Each chapter is a delightful nugget to stimulate the mind and inspire the heart. Bill White has the rare quality of being an authentic and vulnerable man, living in the practical rough and tumble world with the foundations of a thoughtful scholar. His insights into life and Scripture are practical, sensitive, and based in eternal truth.

W. Allen Morris
Chairman & CEO of The Allen Morris Company
Coral Gables, Florida

When I first met Bill, I told him, "I don't like churches, and I don't trust preachers." He told me, "Then we already have something in common." Little did either of us know how both of us would grow through the relationship that began that day . . . a relationship of blessing and adventure like you will read about in his book. I discovered that Bill doesn't just talk the talk; he actually walks the talk. He IS the definition of a true believer, a fact that earned my respect. And he softened my heart.

Al Perkins
Entrepreneur/Outdoorsman
Key West, Florida/Sunset, South Carolina

Bill White does a masterful job in his book, *Upside-Down Kingdom*, of unpacking the Beatitudes with an insightful view towards a life of blessings. Having read the Sermon on the Mount many times, this book offers a different perspective and a path towards Christlikeness. When we apply the four levels of impact described by Bill, God's transformative grace unleashes not only His blessings but also reveals how we can live a life of meaning and purpose. This is a great read for anyone looking to grow spiritually and make a difference in the lives of others.

Sherrie Porter
SVP, General Sales Manager of Berkshire Hathaway HomeServices EWM Realty
Coral Gables, Florida

UPSIDE DOWN KINGDOM

SECRETS OF SPIRITUAL TRANSFORMATION HIDDEN IN THE BEATITUDES

BILL WHITE

ISBNs:
Print: 978-1-947505-22-3
Digital: 978-1-947505-23-0
Cover designed by: Yukiko Centeno, www.akemicreative.com, Miami, FL (Christ Journey Member)
Photography by: Vannia Enriquez & Diego Espinosa, www.flairmiami.com, Miami, FL (Christ Journey Member)
Interior design by Anne McLaughlin, Blue Lake Design
Published by Baxter Press, Friendswood, Texas
Printed in the United States

To

Lisa,

bright and beautiful,

and to what is yet to be

as you have always believed,

"No eye has seen, no ear has heard,

no mind has conceived what God has prepared

for those

who love him."

CONTENTS

Kingdom Adventure

Kingdom Audacity

FOUR LEVELS
OF IMPACT

The Sermon on the Mount has been described as the most powerful message ever spoken. I agree with that assessment, and yet, its power comes in large degree from the surprises woven within Jesus' teaching. The opening section of the sermon is familiar to many people—it's a collection of blessings called "the Beatitudes." But Jesus' idea of blessings is far different from what most of us imagine! I believe He gives us a new measuring stick, a new set of lenses, a new math to help us calculate what's really important in His kingdom. To understand these blessings, we need to learn the new math.

Some years ago, during the rivalry game between Oklahoma University and Oklahoma State, OSU had the ball, but they were six points behind. Time was running out, and they were 80 yards from the goal line . . . in pouring rain. The OSU coach believed the situation was hopeless, so in the spirit of goodwill, he put all the seniors in for the last play of the game so they could end their college football careers on the field. As Randy Johnson, the senior quarterback, ran onto the field wearing his clean jersey, the coach told him, "Call whatever play you want." The team huddled and the quarterback called "Play Thirteen." His teammates were surprised because Play Thirteen had never been called in a game. It was a complicated trick play. They hadn't used it because it had never worked in practice.

But that day the impossible happened, and Play Thirteen worked! OSU scored and quarterback Randy Johnson's team won by one point. As you can imagine, the crowd went wild! As the team carried Randy off the field, his coach shouted to him, "Why in the world did you call Play Thirteen?"

Randy explained, "Well, we're in the huddle, and I look over and see Harry, tears running down his cheeks. It's his last college game and we're losing. I see that big '8' on his chest. Then I see Ralph with tears running down his cheeks. And I see that big '7' on his jersey. So, in honor of those two heartbroken seniors, I added 8 and 7 together and called Play Thirteen."

The coach scratched his head and answered him, "But Randy, seven and eight don't add up to thirteen."

Randy thought for a moment, then said, "You're right, coach. And if I was as smart as you, we wouldn't have won the game!"

In the Beatitudes, Jesus teaches some new math that doesn't seem to add up either. He began His great message with a series of blessings. They declare God's blessing on people's journey through life. Have you ever wanted your family to be blessed by God? Your work? Your marriage? You personally? Have you ever said "God bless you" to somebody? Have you ever had somebody ask you to pray God's blessing for them? What does it mean to be blessed? The Beatitudes show us what blessings look like to Jesus, and He answers the question: What does a life of blessing look like? We'll find surprising answers.

The nine statements show us four levels of impact, first on us and then through us on the lives of those around us. We'll look at Kingdom Access, Kingdom Affluence, Kingdom Adventure, and

Kingdom Audacity. We'll see how these concepts reorient our perspective, rekindle our passion, and redirect our purpose.

Let me share my purpose for writing this book. During the years I've been a pastor, I've found my heart and mind inescapably seized by the Beatitudes in fresh, invigorating, and profound ways. I share some of the insights in this book with the humble and sincere hope that readers will find them to be a tool that helps them move to the next level in their spiritual lives. The path is along the transformational continuum found in the Beatitudes, until, as the Scripture promises, total Christlikeness will be ours in His presence (1 John 3:2).

But how do we grow toward Christlikeness? And what does it look like? How do we know when we've arrived? Does anybody ever really "arrive"? Are there guideposts along the way by which we can mark our progress? You'll find many answers to these crucial questions in the Beatitudes of Jesus recorded in Matthew 5. Read on and enjoy the ride!

This book is designed for individual study and group discussion. You'll find three lessons on each of the nine Beatitudes. If you want to go through the book as a daily devotional, you can use five studies a week for six weeks. I've added a couple of introductory chapters and a summary at the end.

CHAPTER 1

THE NATURE OF GOD'S KINGDOM

For anyone who is even a casual reader of the Bible, it doesn't take long to realize that God's view of things is radically different from ours. We can say that it's actually upside down from our rational expectations. In the pages of Scripture, we find statements like: the way to be great is to be the servant of all; the last shall be first and the first shall be last; to be filled with righteousness you have to admit you have no righteousness at all; true wealth comes from being incredibly generous and giving lots of money away; when I'm weak I'm strong; and many others. Our normal set of values is to reach for as much pleasure, power, and popularity as we can get, but the Bible says that true pleasure is found in God, power is given away, and being accepted by the God of the universe is the only popularity that matters. The Bible challenges us to the core. It forces us to take a long, hard look at our assumptions, expectations, and values, and maybe, just maybe, to ask God to conduct a major work of renovation of our hearts.

We all have times in our lives when conventional wisdom doesn't give us the right answers, and there are times when God's clear directives just don't seem logical. In these moments, we can be perplexed and frustrated, or we can realize it is part of the wonder, the mystery, and the beauty of life. Those moments remind me of the Vulcan Spock or Star Trek's Data: when their logic fails them, then with head tilted and eyebrow raised, they have nothing left to say except, "Fascinating."

This is how I imagine it was for those who first heard Jesus share the Beatitudes. I can almost see their furrowed brows and bewildered curiosity. I can imagine comments like, "Come again?" "Did He say what I *think* He said?" "That doesn't make sense . . ." "Nice poetry. Great for a book on my coffee table. But that's not the way you win this game of life." "What world is He living in? It's sure not mine!"

To illustrate the upside-down nature of God's kingdom, look at this modern summary of the Beatitudes: "God's kind of happiness comes to those who know they are poor. Divine comfort is showered on those whose hearts are broken with grief. If you are truly meek, the whole world belongs to you. And for those of you who are suffering for doing the right thing—Awesome! It's party time! You belong in God's hall of fame!"

To say the Beatitudes of Jesus are counterintuitive is an understatement. The paradoxical truths we find here turn the conventional wisdom of the world on its head. They are totally upside down to the way most of us have learned to think about happiness and success.

Yet here they are—in all their stark contrariness to the ways of the world. But actually, they're truth bombs Jesus explodes to blow away our shackles and liberate us from the myths of the godless superman and invite us to explore the full potential of the life of blessing. Read them again for the very first time.

"Blessed are the poor in spirit,
    for theirs is the kingdom of heaven.
Blessed are those who mourn,
    for they will be comforted.
Blessed are the meek,
    for they will inherit the earth.

Blessed are those who hunger and thirst for righteousness,

for they will be filled.

Blessed are the merciful,

for they will be shown mercy.

Blessed are the pure in heart,

for they shall see God.

Blessed are the peacemakers,

for they will be called sons of God.

Blessed are those who are persecuted because of righteousness,

for theirs is the kingdom of heaven.

Blessed are you when people insult you, persecute you and falsely say all kinds of evil against you because of me. Rejoice and be glad, because great is your reward in heaven, for in the same way they persecuted the prophets who were before you." (Matthew 5:3-12)

The Beatitudes function like a musical staff on which the melody and harmonies of the Spirit are composed. They form a matrix for spiritual development on which personal transformation toward Christlikeness occurs. They are a spiritual growth continuum outlining and highlighting the key elements involved in spiritual maturity against which we can monitor our progress. Jesus' Beatitudes are words of blessing pouring from the heart of our Creator and Redeemer as "deep calls to deep" and invites us to find our way home, where even more blessing is waiting to welcome us.

And they point us to the One who embodies every letter in them.

At the end of each chapter, I invite you to take some time to pray and reflect. Don't skip these steps, and don't rush them. Ask God to speak to you. He may remind you of a passage of Scripture or a particular sentence or two in the chapter, or His Spirit may give you an insight or a nudge to take action. Then, write what God is saying to you, and if He prompts you to do something, do it.

How do you think you would have responded if you'd been one of the first people to hear Jesus when He spoke these unusual blessings?

Describe how the Beatitudes are "upside-down" from our usual expectations of how life works.

What is God saying to you in this chapter?

CHAPTER 2

THE HERO OF
THE BEATITUDES

One of the biggest errors Christians make when they read the Bible, and in this case, the Beatitudes, is to conclude that their obedience and their effort to be like Jesus somehow earns them favor with God. When they make this mistake, they take their eyes off Jesus and His amazing grace and focus on themselves. They spend far more time gazing at their efforts than at the grace Jesus has poured out on them. A misguided gaze inevitably produces one of two results (and often both): pride when they believe they're making good progress and shame when they realize they've failed God's standard again. Christlikeness is the goal of the Christian life, but we never achieve it by focusing on ourselves, our progress, and especially, how well we're doing compared to other people.

Before we dive into the four levels of impact in the nine statements, let's look at the Hero of the Beatitudes.

Jesus became poor in spirit. He stepped out of the splendor of heaven to become the child of poor peasants, flee for His life as an infant, suffer misunderstanding and rejection, and humble himself to die the death we deserved so that we could have the honor He deserves.

Jesus mourned. He wept over the heartache of death at Lazarus's tomb, He wept over the people of Jerusalem who didn't understand that He was giving himself for them, and He was deeply grieved to the point of death as He peered into the abyss of hell in the Garden before His arrest.

Jesus was meek. At the moment of the supreme test of endurance, Jesus asked the Father to let the cup of divine wrath for sin pass from Him, yet He prayed, "Not my will, but yours be done" (Luke 22:42). The Romans and Jewish leaders played bit parts in His crucifixion, but He laid down His life willingly, knowing the enormous cost of suffering.

Jesus hungered and thirsted for righteousness. He was totally dedicated to the Father, and He spent nights in prayer to be close to Him. He taught the truth no matter how He was reviled. On the cross, He said, "I thirst." He got vinegar to drink so that we could drink the cup of love and joy.

Jesus was merciful. Again and again, we see the contrast between the stiff, self-important religious leaders who wouldn't stoop to help those in need, and Jesus tenderly reaching out to care for lepers, the sick, the lame, the blind, the paralyzed, the demon-possessed, and the lost.

Jesus was pure in heart. We see the incredible kindness and patience of Jesus in His interactions with the disciples and those who came to Him for help. And we also see that when He was opposed by the religious leaders, He spoke the truth to them, but He never stooped to their level by sneering at them.

Jesus was a peacemaker. The violence He endured bought peace *with* God so that we escape God's righteous judgment, and now we have the peace *of* God as the Holy Spirit dwells in us and communicates the heart of God to us.

Jesus was persecuted for righteousness sake. He came to seek and to save the lost, and the only way to redeem us was to suffer the most extreme form of torture. He was without sin, but He took on our sin so we could be forgiven and declared righteous—not based on our goodness, but on His.

Jesus endured ridicule. He perfectly represented the Father, but the people who claimed to love God despised Him, plotted to kill Him, falsely accused Him, and gave Him up to the Romans to die.

When we look at the Beatitudes through the lens of Jesus' life, death, and resurrection, we're reminded again of His amazing grace. We deserve nothing, but He gave all. We were helpless and lost, but He came for us and died in our place.

As we look at each of the Beatitudes, remember the Hero. Marvel that He embodies this upside-down kingdom to the fullest extent, and follow Him with your whole heart.

What difference does it make to see Jesus as "the Hero of the Beatitudes" (instead of reading them as only a list of requirements or rules)?

Is Jesus really your Hero? Explain your answer.

What is God saying to you through this chapter?

KINGDOM ACCESS

"Blessed are the poor in spirit,

for theirs is the kingdom of heaven.

Blessed are those who mourn,

for they will be comforted.

Blessed are the meek,

for they will inherit the earth."

(Matthew 5:3-5)

CHAPTER 3

WHEN POVERTY IS PROSPERITY

*"Blessed are the poor in spirit,
for theirs is the kingdom of heaven."*

I admit my need.

The first three beatitudes are about Kingdom Access. This is the first level of impact, and it's about God's impact on you and me. It speaks of our desperate need for God. To gain access to the blessing of knowing and loving God, we need to admit that we have nothing—absolutely nothing—to offer Him, to impress Him, or to twist His arm so He'll accept us. We come empty-handed . . . which means we have to let go of the accomplishments we've trusted in.

Many of us are confused about God's intentions. We might wonder, "If God wants to bless me, then why hasn't He?" Jesus begins by showing us the way to personally access God's kingdom blessing. For most of us, the answer to the question, "Why am I not *experiencing* God's blessing in my life?" may simply be, "You're not *accessing* it yet."

It would be like asking, "Why does God have me sitting in the dark?" Maybe the answer is, "You haven't turned on the light." In the first three beatitudes, I believe Jesus is showing us how to activate the blessing switch.

And I believe that because I've personally experienced it. When I put these first three attitudes in play in my life, they bring God's blessing with them. On the other hand, if these attitudes are absent or lacking, so is my sense of God's blessing.

We could call the first beatitudes *attitudes*. Each one has to do with my sense of personal need and what I do with it:

"Blessed are the poor in spirit": I admit my need.

"Blessed are those who mourn": I grieve my lack.

"Blessed are the meek": I yield my will to God.

We begin at the beginning: "Blessed are the poor in spirit." Many of us—including many who are in church each week—stop in their tracks right here. We don't want admit that we're empty and needy. Instead, we want everyone to see us as competent and good. Admitting our need makes us appear to be flawed and weak, and we can't stand for people to see us that way! But deep in our souls, we know we're not all put together. We wear a mask to present our goodness and competence to the world, but God knows what's in our hearts.

We tell ourselves we're doing just fine, but it's not true. What do you do with your sense of personal need? Do you say, "What need? I'm good. I'm doing all right"? Do you say, "Oh, I *feel* the need, but I'm taking care of it. I'm getting it together"? Or do you say, "Someday I'll get around to being honest with God, but I have things I want to do first. Maybe someday I'll seek His blessing, but right now, I'm my own blessing. Besides, if you compare what I've got going on with others around me, I'm looking pretty good!"?

When we admit our need for God's forgiveness, mercy, and strength, we're being vulnerable with Him. That's essential. We won't make any progress in our spiritual lives as long as we refuse to humble ourselves before Him. Oh, we can make progress in church work by impressing people with our Bible knowledge, our intense emotions in worship, and our generosity, but like the Pharisees, these can all be for show. Church activity isn't the same as a humble heart before God. When we admit we're poor in spirit, we're saying, "I may have trusted in my virtues, but no longer. I admit I'm empty and need to be filled with God's grace, forgiveness, and love."

Admit your need. Take the rational step of seeing the truth about your need for God's magnificent grace. Don't let excuses or pride get in the way. Blessing is on the other side of this door.

What are some reasons people don't want to let down their guard and admit their need?

What are the blessings we experience when we're honest and vulnerable with God?

What is God saying to you through this chapter?

CHAPTER 4

THE CURSE OF COMPARISON

Sometimes we don't think we're needy because we're comparing ourselves to others. We look at the ads in magazines, on television, or online, and we conclude, *I have to have this new gadget, that new car, or the vacation of my dreams to be really happy.* But in reality, we're thinking, *I really need a better gadget, car, and vacation so my friends will be impressed.*

The power of advertising is that it taps into our insatiable thirst for more status, pleasure, and beauty. But the lie of advertising is that these things will bring ultimate fulfillment, when in fact, they satisfy for only a moment, and then we feel empty again. The cycle is never ending: we want more, we expect more, we get more, and we come to the conclusion that whatever we have isn't enough. But instead of realizing this self-destructive pattern and rejecting it, we try even harder to fill our lives with things.

Into this quicksand of comparison and the fear of being left behind, Jesus makes the seemingly absurd comment: "Blessed are the poor in spirit." Let's be clear: He's not glamorizing being poor financially. He's not saying to be close to God we need to take a vow of poverty. There's nothing glamorous about that. But we need to understand the lesson: How do you know you're poor financially? It's simple: Your requirements exceed your resources. You look at your bills, and you look at your income. When what's going out exceeds what's coming in, you rationally conclude, "I'm in need." You have a cognitive awareness of the shortfall, and it registers in your brain, "I'm poor. I'm broke. I don't have what I need." That's a picture of the condition of our souls, and Jesus says that's where the pathway of blessing begins.

One of the people listening to Jesus that day on the hillside was Peter. I love Peter. He was enthusiastic and raw in his devotion to Jesus, but his pride proved to be very costly. At dinner on the last night before Jesus was betrayed, the disciples argued about who would be the greatest in the kingdom they were sure Jesus was going to inaugurate immediately. Their idea of the Messiah was a military leader who would kick the Romans out of Palestine and recreate the nation of Israel. And when that happened, the disciples wanted to be in Jesus' cabinet!

Jesus told them again that He was going to die and they would run away, but Peter insisted, "Even if all fall away on account of you, I never will" (Matthew 26:33). Jesus told him the hard truth that before the night was out, he would deny Him three times. Peter had his own plans that didn't connect with the ones Jesus laid out. Peter had his eye on power and prestige. He was full of himself, but the anguish of his three denials showed him his utter emptiness.

Sometimes, that's what it takes for us, too. We have to come to the end of ourselves—our grand plans, our self-confidence, our vision of personal success—to see that we're empty. Peter learned his lesson. In his first letter a few years later, he wrote, "'God opposes the proud but shows favor to the humble.' Humble yourselves, therefore, under God's mighty hand, that he may lift you up in due time. Cast all your anxiety on him because he cares for you" (1 Peter 5:5-6).

You may be thinking, *All of this is important for people who are investigating faith in Christ, but I've been a Christian for decades. This really doesn't apply to me.* Think again. We never get beyond our desperate need for God's grace. Yes, we enter into a relationship with Him by grace at a point in time, but every moment of every day, we need our motives to be melted and molded by God's love. It's too easy for us to slide back into thinking our good moral choices earn God's love and acceptance. As I read Paul's letters to the churches and to Timothy and Titus, I'm struck by how many times he explains that a deeper grasp of grace is essential for spiritual growth. For instance, in his second letter to the Corinthians, he tells them, "For Christ's love compels us, because we are convinced that one died for all, and therefore all died. And he died for all, that those who live should no longer live for themselves but for him who died for them and was raised again" (2 Corinthians 5:14-15).

In the upside-down kingdom, the way up is first to go down. The way to security is to admit we're insecure. The way to the richness of a deep, intimate love relationship with God is to say, "Lord, I'm nothing, and I have nothing. But I'm all yours."

Do you agree or disagree with the statement: "Comparison kills"? Explain your answer.

How is God's grace an open invitation to "come to the end of ourselves" and trust in Him?

What is God saying to you through this chapter?

CHAPTER 5

THE BLESSINGS OF BANKRUPTCY

All of us want to be successful and happy. It's in our DNA, and it's rooted deep in our national consciousness. The Declaration of Independence claims that the Creator has endowed all of us with "certain unalienable Rights, among these are Life, Liberty and the pursuit of Happiness." Someone said, "Yes, and most Americans have been madly pursuing happiness ever since!" Books on how to be happy abound. Among the titles I discovered not so long ago was *How to Be Happy without Money*. It only costs $19.95. Think about that. You have to pay to learn how to be happy without money!

Most of us have been programmed as good consumers to believe that you can't have happiness without economic means. Jesus disagrees. I'm not advocating that economic poverty is good. It's a blight and hardship, so we work to eradicate poverty and improve the standard of living for all our citizens. It's just that Jesus knows money isn't the secret to success. He explained, "A man's life doesn't consist in the abundance of things he possesses" (Luke 12:15).

Woe to us when we confuse our self-worth with our net worth. But blessings are coming our way when we realize that happiness doesn't depend on stuff. And here's the principle that results in real profits: "Blessed are the poor in spirit, for theirs is the kingdom of heaven." Jesus says that divine bliss, the happiness of heaven, is raining down uniquely on those who know they are poor in spirit. The benefits of God's reign come to those who are convinced they don't have it together—the ones who know and are willing to admit their deficit standing before God. To experience the blessing of God requires us first, then, to acknowledge our utter spiritual bankruptcy.

There were those among Jesus' original hearers who could easily qualify as the spiritually elite of the day. Some were thoroughly schooled in the "things of God"—including the scribes, the Pharisees, the religious leaders. They were rich in knowledge. They had read all the books, including their Scriptures. They were rich in piety and religious rule-keeping. Their strict adherence to the moral and ceremonial demands of "righteousness" was widely known. They were sure that being a rule-keeper was the key to God's blessing. To these listeners, Jesus' first beatitude sounded like heresy.

The blessings of God, according to Jesus, aren't for those who can claim bragging rights to spiritual superiority in any way, shape, or form. The riches of heaven are only offered to those who know exactly the opposite to be true about themselves. They have the insight and courage to admit they're morally, ethically, and spiritually bankrupt. Not Chapter 11 reorganization, but Chapter 7 liquidation—it's hopeless . . . it's over . . . even scandalously so. Those who really understand their true condition would call themselves the "spiritually challenged" or the "righteousness impaired."

Amazingly, Jesus insists, "If that's you, then God's kingdom is open to you!" There is no elitism in Jesus' kingdom, and no requirement of prior righteousness. The playing field is level. Nobody gets moved to the front of the line because they're better than somebody else. God's blessings aren't earned, deserved, merited, or achieved in any way. They can only be received. That's why it's called *amazing* grace . . . *marvelous* grace . . . even *scandalous* grace. And Jesus' kingdom is built on it. It forms the welcome mat of heaven. It's the way into the kingdom.

And yet, something in us resists and rebels at the thought of being deficient. We would rather prove our worthiness. Other religious systems are built on some kind of performance plan by which followers can merit or manipulate divine favor. It's human nature to try to work hard, be good, and earn God's love . . . but it's spiritually deadly.

What do you sense in your heart right now? Are you thinking, *Yeah, but I've worked so hard. I've tried to be a good spouse and parent. I've given and served and sacrificed. Don't these count for anything?* As a means of salvation and security in God's kingdom, no, they don't count, and in fact, they're barriers to your experience of grace. After we humble ourselves and admit we're poor in spirit, we become rich in grace and do the same things, but now out of gratitude. The actions may be the same, but the motivation is diametrically different.

Or do you sense that the first beatitude is the good and right starting point for you to be touched by the heart of God? Are you amazed that Jesus was fabulously rich but became poor—in material wealth and in social status—so He could fill our lives with the blessings of His great love?

That's what this beatitude is about.

What are some signs that people (like you and me) confuse our self-worth with our net worth?

What are the blessings of admitting we're spiritually bankrupt? Why is it so hard to admit this? Why is it necessary?

What is God saying to you through this chapter?

CHAPTER 6

GODLY SORROW

"Blessed are those who mourn, for they will be comforted."

I grieve my lack.

The first beatitude is the rational step to admit our need for God's grace; the second one is the emotional step of grieving our moral failures. Some of us don't like to admit it, but God has made us emotional creatures. How we feel about something is often more compelling than our opinions or convictions about it. Our perceptions trigger powerful chemicals in the brain, which then creates strong emotions. Dopamine is the pleasure trigger. It rewards doing good with feeling good. This, of course, makes us want to do it again. Serotonin is important in regulating our mood—easing depression when it's in balance, or causing depression, anxiety, and anger when it's not. Norepinephrine also controls stress and anxiety.

The rational perception that we're spiritually bankrupt causes us to mourn our condition. The discovery of the gaping hole in our hearts isn't something we take lightly. If we realize the depth of our selfishness, our impure motives, and our desire to use people instead of loving them, our hearts hurt. We grieve over our sins. Grief can either crush us under the weight of self-pity and shame, or it can point us to the One who loves, forgives, and accepts.

This is the point of repentance. Some believe repentance happens only at the time we trust in Jesus, but actually we remain flawed people even after we're forgiven and declared righteous in God's sight. I believe Jesus is teaching that we need to develop the habit of repenting. When Martin Luther nailed the 95 Theses to the church door in Wittenberg in 1517, the first one on the list read: "When our Lord and Master Jesus Christ said, 'Repent' (Mt 4:17), he willed the entire life of believers to be one of repentance." Don't miss that: "the entire life."

Actually, there are two kinds of repentance. In his second letter to the Corinthians, Paul describes them both. The church in Corinth had a lot of problems. They bickered with each other and jockeyed for positions of power. They had sexual problems, pride problems, theological problems, leadership problems, and relational problems. Paul's earlier letter had called them out, and for a while, he wondered how they had received his rebuke. Then, he got word of their response, and he wrote back to them:

> Even if I caused you sorrow by my letter, I do not regret it. Though I did regret it—I see that my letter hurt you, but only for a little while— yet now I am happy, not because you were made sorry, but because your sorrow led you to repentance. For you became sorrowful as God intended and so were not harmed in any way by us. Godly sorrow brings repentance that leads to salvation and leaves no regret, but worldly sorrow brings death. See what this godly sorrow has produced in you: what earnestness, what eagerness to clear yourselves, what indignation, what alarm, what longing, what concern, what readiness to see justice done. (2 Corinthians 7:8-11)

Godly sorrow is the kind of repentance Luther was talking about. It connects us with the heart of God, reminds us that His forgiveness is sufficient for every sin, no matter how dark, and refreshes us in His love. In stark contrast, *worldly sorrow* is beating ourselves up for being so bad, groveling in self-pity, trying to do enough penance to make up for our sin, and being overwhelmed by the shame of never measuring up.

The second beatitude invites godly sorrow. With it, we're deeply touched—not only by the depth of our need, but also by the height of God's love and forgiveness. This kind of mourning is essential if we want to know Christ, follow Christ, and become more like Christ.

How would you contrast "godly sorrow" with "worldly sorrow"? What are the results of each?

Are you skilled at the art of repentance? Explain your answer.

What is God saying to you through this chapter?

CHAPTER 7

GOOD GRIEF

For some of us, it's very hard to believe that God forgives us. Some time ago, a friend shared with me about a visit he had made to the hospital to visit a young woman who had been a student at the school where he taught. She had an eating disorder that had robbed her of much of her life. Her bones showed through her jeans, and her eyelids drooped. Her condition had gotten so serious that she had to be hospitalized. My friend surprised her with a visit and some flowers. Her mother was in the room, but she walked outside to let them talk. He told his former student that he knew very little about anorexia, but he knew that it's a difficult, complex problem. He knew that she had been struggling with it for a long, long time.

In a burst of vulnerability, she told him, "I've always thought of myself as an honest person, but I hide behind lies and deception." She said she had grown up desiring to be genuine. "And I've been so active in my church. You know, I even teach Sunday school to elementary children." She told him about times with the therapist, about the war within herself, and about what triggered it. She explained that she was terribly offended when nurses encouraged her to "Eat more." Then she thought back to a crucial relationship. She told him how she could never seem to please her grandmother. Her grandmother's refusal to accept her reached into the core of her problem.

At one point, my friend said it just felt right to call her by name and say, "I don't know a lot, but I know you've got to let things go. Two thousand years ago, God loved you so much that He sent Christ to die for your sins, the ones in the past, the ones today, and even the ones you'll commit tomorrow. He forgave you and me, and He believes in you now. I know that one of the best things anyone can do for healing is to forgive others. You bring healing on yourself that way." He paused for a second, and then continued. "For one, you need to forgive those nurses. They should know better but they don't. They're simply trying to help you and make you better. And your grandmother . . . she is who she is and probably did what she thought was best. You've got to let go of your resentment and forgive her. You need to pass on the forgiveness you've received from Christ to all of them and move on."

They talked for well over an hour. He didn't really remember much else of what they talked about. But when he left, her mother said to him, "Look at her face. She hasn't smiled that way in a long time."

What kind of smile was it? Maybe the smile of being loved . . . of being accepted. Maybe it was the smile of truth, of coming out of the darkness of hiding and into the fellowship of forgiveness.

What do you do with the pain in your life when you can't hide it or run away from it any longer . . . when you can't drink it away, drug it away, or deny it away anymore . . . when it becomes impossible to ignore it or cover it up one more day?

This is one of the most important questions for us, isn't it? And Jesus gives us His answer in the second beatitude. It is extremely significant because it helps us deal with the pain in our lives. Jesus said, "Blessed are those who mourn, for they will be comforted."

When I studied this verse, I wondered, *Did this sound as strange to those who first heard it as it does to me? How can there be blessing in grieving life's deepest losses? Happiness doesn't come from sadness. Everybody knows that. Besides, I look at the world, I read the headlines, I see the news: war, famine, disease, floods, fires, sexual assault, suicide, and on and on. We live in a world of hurt with millions in crisis, and they seem to be living without much comfort.*

Actually, things weren't all that different when Jesus first spoke these words. Surely there were those in the crowd that day doubled over with sorrow. Some were so grief stricken that they wondered if they were going to make it. Some had lost loved ones: parents, spouses, friends, even children. Some hearts were breaking as Jesus spoke. And some were so overcome with sadness that they felt they were beyond consolation.

In spite of how things seemed, Jesus was telling them, "If you are burdened with grief and sorrow, I have some good news for you: It doesn't matter the depth of your pain and the scope of your problem. It doesn't matter how beaten up or broken down you feel. Blessing is coming your way! You're accepted and your pain is welcome here. Come in, lay your burden down, and be comforted. In My kingdom every broken heart can find mending and every weary soul can find relief."

Jesus is saying to people anguishing in turmoil and grief, "There is a soothing balm close at hand. The happiness of heaven is being showered down on those mourning the loss of things they held precious, and the comfort of God is drawing near." This promise isn't superficial. This is deep. This is real.

Some of you will know what I mean when I say, "God meets us close at the wound." He has an affinity for broken people and broken places. When my youngest daughter Jessica was a preschooler, she would bring her baby doll to me, leg in one hand, and the rest of the doll in the other, and she would say, "Yeg off. Pitzit, Daddy," which translated means "Leg off. Fix it, Daddy." Instinctively, she felt that in her father's hands, the broken place could be restored. Jesus is sharing the same truth with us in this beatitude.

Life hurts. There are times when things precious to us fall to pieces in our hands. Life can be extremely painful. What are we to do with the pain? Two things. I'll address one in this chapter and the other in the next one. Let me state them in the first person. First, I am to let my pain touch me . . . let it move me.

You're probably thinking, *That's ludicrous. I'm trying to get away from my pain! The last thing I'm going to do is embrace it.* I understand that sentiment. It's one I relate to personally. So can the apostle Paul. When confronted with the pain of that mysterious "thorn in the flesh" (2 Corinthians 12:7), he wanted it to be gone! In fact, three times he pleaded with God to take it away. If the Super Saint Paul didn't want to face his pain, how much more do I want to run away from mine? Yet Jesus says the blessing doesn't only come from the removal of suffering; there is blessing in the mourning over suffering.

This is an emotional beatitude. The word translated *mourning* is the strongest word for grief and sorrow in the Greek language. Jesus is saying, "Don't be afraid to feel the sadness, to let your emotions flow." Emotions are the oil of life. They help the gears mesh and move.

Jesus is promising, "Don't be afraid. Your feelings are safe with Me." Have you ever had a friend in whose presence you were totally safe to share your deepest feelings of pain? Jesus is that kind of friend.

Jesus wasn't beyond being touched emotionally. When He saw the crowds, His heart went out to them, and He was moved with deep feeling (Matthew 9:36). When He stood at the graveside of a loved one, tears welled up in His eyes and streamed down His face (John 11:35).

Our grief might be more than personal. As Jesus came into Jerusalem, the desperate spiritual condition of the city moved Him to weep openly (Luke 19:11). Maybe you are similarly saddened as you reflect on the shape our society is in. It concerns you. It moves you. Jesus was moved emotionally by the needy condition of his home-land. He was an emotional man. He didn't hide from His pain. When He was hanging on the cross, they brought Him wine mixed with gall as a narcotic to deaden the pain, but He refused it (Matthew 27:34). Jesus wasn't afraid of pain. And He's telling us we don't have to be either.

Mourning is a part of life because sometimes things happen that hurt us deeply. Jesus is saying, "You don't have to numb up. You don't have to grow calloused and harden your heart to survive. You don't have to play denial games or think you're all alone. In My kingdom, people in pain don't go it alone. There is another way we deal with it. Come to Me. Pour out your pain and heartache. I understand. I love you. I'm with you."

We often think of grief only in the context of disease and death. Why is it important to grieve *all* our losses? What are some of your losses?

Who is someone you know who is good at grieving (that is, being honest about the pain without slipping into self-pity)? What can you learn from that person?

What is God saying to you through this chapter?

CHAPTER 8

THE PROBLEM OF PAIN

The beatitude about mourning also teaches us a second lesson: When pain touches me, I should let it take me to God. Pain is never fun. My family has known the pain of loneliness, rejection, bereavement, financial reversal and hardship, and disease. You probably have, too. How about the loss of a job? A failed marriage? A family in turmoil? Do you ever wonder where God is when it seems everything is going wrong?

The Bible says He's closer than your breath: "In him we live and move and have our being" (Acts 17:28). "The Lord is close to the brokenhearted and saves those who are crushed in spirit" (Psalm 34:18). Not only is He near, the Scriptures claim God is feeling your pain. The writer to the Hebrews tells us that God is "touched by the feeling of our infirmities" (Hebrews 4:15 KJV). Think about that for a moment. Right this second, the infinite, almighty God is feeling your pain. He's sensing every sting and sharing in every heartache in your life. God isn't distant, aloof, removed from the dirty business of real life in the trenches. He's not somewhere off in the cosmos twiddling His omnipotent thumbs. He's involved. He's touched by your pain. He's close to those who suffer.

So we instinctively ask, "Then why doesn't He do something?" And the answer is, "But He has." In Christ, God has personally entered into our suffering. As the God-Man, He has forever united eternity and time in Christ. He knows in the forever present tense what it feels like to lose His closest friends, to be ridiculed and humiliated, to suffer unjustly, to bleed, and to die. He knows what it means to feel utterly alone and misunderstood. The Father knows what it's like to lose a beloved Son. Believe me, He's not far from you in your pain.

We still ask, "But why doesn't He do something today?" The answer is, "But He has!" He sent us His Holy Spirit, the Comforter, to encourage and strengthen and console us. He gave us His family, the church, to be a community of comfort to us. This is the place where we learn to love and be loved in joy and in sorrow, where we "weep with those who weep" (Romans 12:15 KJV).

I have conducted uncounted memorial services as a pastor. One of them, for a young woman named Yetty, happened the very week I was preparing to teach this beatitude at our church. Over 800 people were at her service. Some were part of our church family, but several hundred were not. Together we shared the comfort of the Holy Spirit, the good news of Jesus Christ, and the love of God's people speaking the language of the heart. The presence of God was beyond words. Yetty's testimony was powerful. She was a beautiful vivacious young woman, a sweet sister, a cherished wife, a beloved mother. She had received Christ as her personal Savior in 1996. The next day she was told she had terminal cancer. She went to heaven in July of 1998, but not before she had invited hundreds of people to go with her and experience the divine favor of this beatitude: "Blessed are those who mourn for they will be comforted." What a mighty God we serve!

You wonder, "But why doesn't God do something to stop the suffering?" That's a good question, and I'm not exactly sure what the answer is. I know it has something to do with not violating our freedom and autonomy and that consequences must accompany our choices if we are to be truly free. But in a very practical sense, I wonder if it isn't also the fact that, in our pride and stubborn rebellion, some of us never look up until we're flat on our backs. If it weren't for the pain and suffering we encounter, we would never experience the God of eternal comfort.

Jesus knows us, Jesus knows human nature, and Jesus knows life. He knows that God's purpose is far greater than simply the removal of pain. God's purpose is the redemption of your soul and the transformation of your values and relationships. Sometimes the process involves pain, much like a surgeon must cut in order to heal.

In the Parable of the Prodigal Son, Jesus makes it clear that it wasn't until the younger brother had exhausted all his resources and was belly up in suffering and humiliation that he had his first thought about going home. It hadn't even entered his mind until that point. But somehow in the pain of that pig sty, the young man "came to his senses" (Luke 15:17) and decided to head for home. He had a nice little speech polished and carefully rehearsed: "Father, I have sinned against heaven and against you. I am no longer worthy to be called your son; make me one of your hired men" (vs. 18-19). But when he got home, his dad didn't even let him finish his lines. His son barely arrived on the scene when suddenly a new robe was thrown over his shoulders, fresh steaks were thrown on the grill, and his dad threw a party to celebrate his return.

Why am I sharing that story? Because it answers the most important question: How do we get in on the comfort of God? Here's the answer: Come home to the Father with your poverty and your pain. This is what the first two beatitudes tell us: God's blessing comes to those who are poor in spirit and in a state of mourning. In other words, you have to be perceptive enough to know you need God and sensitive enough to feel your loss without Him. You say to God, "Lord, I need you. I know it in my head. I feel it in my heart. And I'm sorry for the shape I'm in, but I'm bringing my pain to You. I've got to have some relief!"

Let me be blunt: Don't buy the snake oil of feel-good Christianity. Some pastors and teachers promise that if you turn to God, He'll make you feel happy all the time. But Jesus is saying, "Turn to God because He's the truth, because you must and you should. And if you do, know this: Life is still going to hurt, but you will never go uncomforted. There will be times you feel like damaged goods, when discouragement threatens to swallow you whole. But you'll discover that just beyond the pain is the presence of God, your Comforter."

No one is beyond God's reach. No pain is beyond God's relief. No crisis exceeds God's comfort. Corrie ten Boom reported her sister Betsie's words before she died in a Nazi concentration camp during the Holocaust: "No pit is so deep that God is not deeper still." Whatever your pain, stop hiding. Bring it home to God. His comforting embrace awaits you.

What piercing questions have you asked God during times of pain and loss? What eventually brought comfort?

In what way is grief a choice, and in what way is it a process?

What is God saying to you through this chapter?

CHAPTER 9

THE NECESSARY STEP

"Blessed are the meek, for they will inherit the earth."

I yield my will.

On the face of it, this beatitude sounds about as exciting as watching paint dry. Besides the apparent boredom factor, those of us who have lived for a while take one look at this, and a game show reject buzzer goes off in our heads: "Nnnnnght! Thanks for playing, but that's not the way the world works." Most people believe that the meek don't inherit the earth; the spoils go to the strong. Meekness is weakness. Just ask Darwin. It's called "the survival of the fittest," and only the strong survive. If you truly want to get anywhere in this world, you must assert yourself and increase your power over others. Be ruthless, be fierce, and never let anyone see you sweat. At least, that's what most people believe.

Maybe you've seen an ad like the one I received in the mail. The opening header reads: "Twenty days to power, influence, and control over people. Our approach gives you power over others and makes them provide you with everything you want in life." (Now we're talking!) It continues, "Dear Friend, take a good look at yourself in the mirror. Make it a farewell look. In a few weeks an entirely new person—an astonishingly more powerful person is going to appear before your eyes." Then it goes through the days, explaining what is going to happen during my twenty days of power. Days 8 through 14 sound especially delicious, "Here's where tough bosses, obstinate customers and clients, stubborn authorities and anyone else who's been holding you back from big money and success finally get put in their place. Now it's your turn. From here on, you get your way at last!"

Sound enticing? I decided to pass. Actually, I consider this type of advertising to be an insult. It takes something good, the ambition to lead a productive and successful life, and marries it to manipulation and behaviors that injure others and put them down. Jesus says, "It doesn't have to be that way. There is another way to success. In My kingdom the blessing of success isn't the sole providence of the high and mighty, the rich and famous, the type A personalities, or the 'Do unto others before they do unto you' kind of people who scrape, claw, and climb on and over others to reach the top."

Jesus says divine blessing comes to those who know how, when, and where to yield. Your standing in His kingdom isn't determined by your ability to compete or manipulate. This is quite different from our world and the madness that spawns so-called "reality TV" shows built on competition, deception, manipulation, and rejection. Jesus says the happiness of heaven and the fullness of the earth are promised to the very people the world considers disempowered, marginalized, and without influence. It's as if He's saying, "Yield to God and He'll take care of you. Your inheritance is secure. You don't have connections? Don't worry about it. God's got your number, and He's making you an heir to His good earth."

Why is the attitude of yielding so special to God? Because it's the antithesis of arrogant pride. Meekness is the willingness to yield. We'll unpack that more in a moment, but first let's list a few things meekness is not. Meekness is not weakness. It's not a kind of milque-toast or treat-me-like-a-doormat mentality. Meekness isn't cowardice that gives in to every strong breeze of others' opinions. Being meek doesn't mean we should be tepid, dispassionate, or wimpy. One of the reasons the gospel seems unattractive to many is because it's perceived in this way. Like the story of the vitamin salesman: scrawny in appearance—he looked like a piece of skin pulled over a bone—yet he stood at the customer's door waxing eloquent about the benefits of this multi-strength daily supplement vitamin. When he finished his pitch, his customer only had one question. "Do you take them?"

There is some truth in saying that some of us are going to have to look more saved if we're really going be God's partners in saving the world. Somebody said, "If the meek are really going to inherit the earth, they're going to have to be more assertive."

What am I trying to say? Meekness isn't a negative; it's a positive. Meekness isn't timidity, it's humility. Meekness means yielding control. The word is used in another context to describe a stallion yielded to the reins of a worthy rider. The story of the horse, Seabiscuit, is a story about meekness. Seabiscuit wasn't a promising race horse—he was small, won very few races at the start of his racing career, and was seriously injured—but he yielded to the purchase of a new owner, yielded to the direction of a new trainer, and yielded to the reins of a new jockey . . . and did what nobody ever thought possible. He somehow kept winding up in the Winner's Circle. Talk about a reversal of fortune!

This is God's plan for each of us. We yield to the purchase of our new owner, God the Father, who has bought us with a price. "You are not your own; you were bought at a price. Therefore, honor God with your body" (1 Corinthians 6:19-20). We yield to the instruction of our new trainer, God the Son, who is our mentor and model in all things. "I have set for you an example that you should do as I have done for you. I tell you the truth, no servant is greater than his master, nor is a messenger greater than the one who sent him. Now that you know these things you will be blessed if you do them" (John 13:15-17). And we yield to the reign and reins of our new rider, God the Holy Spirit, who lives inside us to lead and to guide us. Jesus told His disciples to expect the coming ministry of the Spirit of Truth, the Comforter and Counselor, the Holy Spirit the Father would be sending them: "He lives with you and will be in you . . . When he, the Spirit of truth, comes, he will guide you into all truth (John 14:17, 16:13). Just as a powerful and spirited horse would be considered "meek" when yielded to a trainer or rider, we are meek when we yield to God's mastery over us. Meekness isn't the absence of initiative or strength; it's the yielding of strength to God's leadership and control.

You receive your ticket to the world when you yield control of your life to God. The earth becomes your oyster when God becomes your Master. Meekness is knowing who God is and who you are, in that order. It's the same experience the writer of the Proverbs communicated: "The fear of the Lord is the beginning of wisdom" (Proverbs 1:7). The reverent obedience of a God-controlled spirit brings the blessing of divine inheritance into your life. And it's the polar opposite of stubborn, hardheaded human pride.

Meekness is an affront to human pride and arrogance. That was true when Jesus first declared it, and it's no less so today. The Jews had a pride of race; the Romans, their pride of power; the Greeks, their pride of knowledge. Jesus says it is not race, power, or knowledge that are the keys to true security and success—it's submission to God.

What is God asking us to yield to Him?

What is He specifically asking *you* to yield to Him?

What is God saying to you through this chapter?

CHAPTER 10

IS MEEKNESS A WEAKNESS?

Growing up in Arizona and pastoring in Texas for several years, I had ample opportunity to acquire my own sense of what is known as "cowboy pride." You may not know it, but cowboys sometimes write poetry. One of my favorites is entitled "Typical" by Waddie Mitchell.

Typical

He was out on the cliff's edge; further than he'd ever been before.
He sat with legs a-danglin' high above the valley floor.
He was lost in thought while drinkin' in the grandeur of it all,
When a gust of wind unseated him, and he began to fall.
Tis a drastic situation! He didn't dare to think slow
For certain death awaited him on those rocky crags below.
So… Well.. He called upon a good friend. I guess the only one
   he could.
The one we all forget about when things are going good.
"God, if you help me now I'll quit my sinful ways.
I'd do the things you'd have me do and I'll work hard all my days!
I'll spend time with my children; I'll help my lovin' wife.
I'll quit the booze and whiskey and I'll turn around my life.
I'll work to help the needy and I'll promise to repent…

Just then a tree limb caught his coat and stopped his fast descent. And while hanging from that tree that grew out of that rocky shelf, He looked skyward saying, "Never mind! I handled it myself!"[1]

Does that sound typical to you? Meekness . . . humility . . . submission . . . yielding . . . often feels like weakness to us because we're so deluded by the myth of macho, the "I did it my way" cult of self-worship. Listen, nobody, not Sinatra, not Elvis, *nobody* ever enters heaven singing "I did it my way."

But by the same token, if we are deluded about the ineffective power of self-reliance in the spiritual realm, we are just as much in the dark about the power of Spirit-reliance because we have precious little experience in yielding to God's strength. God's strength is what you tap into when you yield to Spirit-reliance. The Bible is full of stories of people who learned how to succeed in life by yielding to God.

Did you know that Moses is called the meekest man to ever live? The King James Version translates Numbers 12:3 this way, "Now the man Moses was very meek, above all the men who were upon the face of the earth." Yet it was this man who faced down the mighty Pharaoh. It was this man who raised his staff in front of the Red Sea and watched the waters part. It was this man who brought the Ten Commandments down from God on the holy mountain. It was this man who led the multitudes of doubting, obstinate people through the wilderness for forty years. Through Moses' meekness, his willingness to yield to God, a nation was delivered from slavery and led to the Land of Promise. It wasn't the pride of "I'll do it my way," or "Never mind, Lord, I'll handle it myself." It was the humble submission of a man to the will of God.

In Matthew 11:29, in a poignant moment of self-disclosure, Jesus says, "I am meek and lowly of heart" (KJV). Yet Jesus went toe to toe with the self-righteous Pharisees, and He turned over the tables of the moneychangers in the temple. Jesus outlived and out-died every other person in human history, and by His death and resurrection, He made possible the redemption of the world. How? Through His meekness.

Meekness isn't weakness. Meekness is the poise of God showing up in a ravenous world bent on violence and destruction. Meekness accesses the blessing of God even when it looks like all is lost. Meekness promises hope in the midst of despair, because meekness realizes the promise of God's presence and power in our circumstances.

Our primeval parents, Adam and Eve, were swindled out of the original deed to the earth in their temptation and fall into sin. But now in Christ, those who yield get to experience God reverse the curse and restore the original inheritance. Psalm 37:9-11 reminds us that God is at work in spite of the wickedness in the world: "Evil men will be cut off, but those who hope in the Lord will inherit the land. A little while and the wicked will be no more; though you look for them, they will not be found. But the meek will inherit the land and enjoy great peace."

How are we to let God reverse the curse in our lives? How do we get in on the blessings of His promises coming to pass in this world? By taking a crucial step.

Describe the kind of inner strength it takes to be truly meek.

Who is someone you admire who has enough inner composure and confidence to be truly humble? What's so attractive about that person?

What is God saying to you through this chapter?

CHAPTER 11

TAKE THE STEP

In *Alice's Adventures in Wonderland,* a rabbit hole takes Alice into Wonderland. In C.S. Lewis's *The Lion, The Witch and the Wardrobe,* Lucy enters into the magical world of Narnia through an old wardrobe. In the movie series *The Matrix,* Morpheus, Trinity, and Neo access a computerized alternative reality by a modem. These are ways to step into a new reality. Jesus offers one that's very different from the rest: The way we enter the kingdom of heaven is through the meekness of repentance and faith.

The first message Jesus preached in the Gospel of Mark was simply this, "The time has come. The kingdom of God has come near. Repent and believe the good news!" (Mark 1:15) What does it mean to repent and believe? Jesus shows us in the first three beatitudes: There are three distinct elements: a rational one, an emotional one, and a volitional one. These three combine to provide an open door into the journey of spiritual transformation awaiting every Christ-follower.

The first element is a rational awareness and acknowledgement of personal spiritual need: "Blessed are the poor in spirit for theirs is the kingdom of heaven." In other words, *I admit my need.*

The word translated "poor" is an accounting term and simply means I have done an inventory of my spiritual life and found myself wanting. The kingdom of heaven—the blessing of life under God's rule—is for those who know they are spiritually destitute . . .

completely bankrupt . . . those who admit, "I'm deficient when it comes to my standing before God."

This is the kind of really good news that sometimes sounds like bad news at the same time. The really good news is that in heaven's eyes, nobody is beyond the hope and help of God. The blessed reign of God is available to all, especially those considered most hopeless from a human point of view. Nobody is beyond the reach of grace— not the marginalized, the rejected, the not-quite-good-enoughs from the world's perspective, or the losers.

In his book, *Divine Conspiracy,* Dallas Willard corrects a common misunderstanding of the Beatitudes as conditions of merit by which we are to achieve a state of blessing. Instead, he sees them as a demonstration of the radical inclusivity of Jesus' kingdom for people willing to acknowledge their desperate need before God. Jesus is the Friend of sinners for those ready to admit they need forgiveness. Willard paraphrases the first beatitude, "Blessed are the spiritual zeros—the spiritually bankrupt, deprived and deficient, the spiritual beggars, those without a wisp of 'religion'—when the kingdom of heaven comes upon them."[2] Those he lists among the poor in spirit in today's world are: "The flunk-outs and drop-outs and burned outs. The drug heads and divorced. The HIV-positive and herpes ridden. The brain damaged, the incurably ill. The barren and the pregnant too many times or at the wrong time. The overemployed, the underemployed, the unemployed. The unemployable. The swindled, the shoved aside, the replaced. The parents with children living on the street, the children with parents not dying in the 'rest' home. The lonely, incompetent, the stupid. The emotionally starved or emotionally dead . . . the moral disasters."[3]

These are the ones who know they don't have it all together . . . the ones honest enough to admit their lives are in pieces. Do you qualify?

If you do, I've got good news: Jesus is a Friend of sinners! The sign over the entrance to the kingdom is like a huge billboard with bright lights shining on it. It reads, "If you're willing to admit you're poor in spirit, you're welcome here!" God brings us to the end of ourselves that He might display His sufficiency.

The second element is an emotional one, "Blessed are those who mourn for they shall be comforted." Mourn what? The context seems to indicate their poverty of spirit. In other words, I not only rationally understand my need for God, I'm also aware of its emotional pain. The pain is real. *I grieve my lack.*

Repentance means I know something's not right in me, and I feel bad about it. I feel the pain of my brokenness, and it moves me. I'm emptied of myself, and I understand that I cannot save myself. This kind of repentance embraces the grace of God, relishes His forgiveness, and "leaves no regret" (2 Corinthians 7:10). Think about that. How would you like to come to the end of your days, look back over your life, and have no regret? You may be thinking, *It's too late. I've got all kinds of regrets.* Jesus is saying it's never too late if you're willing to admit your need, feel its pain, and become ready and willing for a change.

Jesus told His followers He would send a Comforter, His Holy Spirit, to encourage and counsel them. In John 16:7-11, Jesus tells us that the Spirit convicts us of our guilt, (part of the Spirit's role is to help us feel our poverty of spirit before God), then guides us to the righteousness of Christ to meet our need. He comforts us as we are moved to come to God and we're ready to take the third step. *I yield my will.*

This third element is volitional. I choose God's will for me before I even know what it is. Remember, meek doesn't mean shy, reserved, or unassertive. It means yielding control like a stallion yields to the reins of a rider and is ridden to the Winner's Circle.

Jesus is saying that those who yield to God will find the pieces of their world coming together. The psalmist assures us that God will show himself mighty to protect and deliver, and He'll keep His promises no matter how bad things seem. He steps in to reverse the curse of sin and restore the blessings of life (Psalm 37). The Bible teaches that the earth and all its fullness is the Lord's (Psalm 24:1). He gave it to Adam and Eve to enjoy and develop, but they lost it. But now in Christ, God begins the process of restoring our original inheritance. We can experience what Paul describes as "having nothing, and yet possessing everything" (2 Corinthians 6:10).

This is an invitation to let God have you. Offer all that you are to all that He is. Hold nothing back, and you will enter the kingdom and begin (or continue) your transformation experience. The steps are clear, challenging, and full of promise: admit your need, grieve your lack, and yield your will to the King of kings.

Before we go any further in this journey, it's time for you to stop and ask God to make real in your life the truths we have been discovering. Will you join me in prayer right now? Place your hand on your heart and say out loud to God:

Lord, I need You. I admit it. I'm in a spiritually deficit position. Rationally, I admit I'm a sinner. I have thought, said, and done things that I should not have. I have left unsaid and undone many things that I should not have. Spiritually, I'm in the red. I'm broke, Lord, I don't have it together. The truth is that "Chapter 7" accurately describes my spiritual and moral condition. And I feel it.

My hand on my heart right now is my way of asking You to let me feel it even more, so I gladly turn to You. Help me grieve the problems I've caused by my selfishness and sin. I'm so sorry for the injury I've caused myself and others, and for how I've dishonored You. Forgive me, Lord, for running away from my pain and for not running to You with it. I'm coming to You ready for a change in my life. Please, forgive me and be my Comforter.

I now yield all of me to You. I yield my will, my problems, my failures, my hopes, and my dreams. I give all that I know about me to all that I know about You. Lord, I make You my King, and I choose Your will for my life—right now, before I even know what it is. Come into my life and lead me in the way You would have me go. I place myself at Your disposal because I believe You love me and have my best interest at heart.

Thank You for Your promise of unconditional grace in Christ. Thank You for Jesus and His death and resurrection for me. I now receive Your kingship and management over my life. I receive Your comfort and forgiveness. I receive the inheritance You promised for me in this life and the next. In Jesus' name I pray, amen.

If transformation is your aim, then nothing less than a prayer of this breadth and depth of surrender will do. If you feel this is premature to your journey at this point, maybe this prayer will serve: "Lord, if You are real, show yourself to me. Take me to the next level in my journey with You. Open my eyes. Soften my heart. Help me become willing to be willing to yield."

And if you've already trusted Christ at some point in your life, you can pray, "Lord, I need this reminder. Thank You for drawing me back, again and again, to the wonder of Your grace. Today, again, I admit my need to experience Your love and forgiveness more deeply, I grieve my selfishness and the ways I've hurt others, and I yield to You as my sovereign King. Work Your grace, love, and power deep within me."

This is the faith step of real repentance. This is the decision that opens the door to spiritual transformation and personal life change. And this is the step of repentance and faith we take again and again to keep our relationship with God fresh and strong.

Have you taken the step of faith, realizing you can't earn God's love but you can receive it as a free gift? If you have, what brought you to that point? If you haven't, is this the right time to take that step?

Why do we need constant reminders about God's grace, love, and strength?

What is God saying to you through this chapter?

KINGDOM AFFLUENCE

"Blessed are those who hunger and thirst for

righteousness,

for they will be filled.

Blessed are the merciful,

for they will be shown mercy.

Blessed are the pure in heart,

for they shall see God." (Matthew 5:6-8)

CHAPTER 12

A HEALTHY APPETITE

"Blessed are those who hunger and thirst
for righteousness, for they will be filled."

I experience God's life.

All living things have appetites . . . ours are just a little more complicated than those of other life forms. We hunger and thirst for pleasure,
for prosperity, or for power—and the more we get, the more we want.
At a deeper level, we want to love and be loved, to feel secure and to
have a life full of meaning. The Rolling Stones told us that we "can't get
no satisfaction." Twenty years later they released "You Can't Always
Get What You Want." Am I detecting a pattern here? Our hungers are
legitimate, but we usually feed them with spiritual junk food.

Into that sad condition, Jesus offers this perspective: blessing
comes when we hunger and thirst for righteousness. But to be clear,
this righteousness is not a list of "right" things we must do to be filled.
Jesus isn't speaking of self-righteousness in attitude or action. The
kind of righteousness He's describing is "right standing" with God.
It's a status that can't be reduced or cancelled, and it makes us long
to live up to our new identity. That's part of the wonder of His grace.

What are you hungry and thirsty for? Where are you looking to find satisfaction? The blessings of satisfaction and fullness only come when you are hungry to have a right standing with the Father. Here's the truth: God offers this blessing when we belong to Him.

There's a reason people talk about having a healthy appetite; it's because a good appetite is a sign we're healthy and alive. How's this for a paraphrase for this beatitude: "Mmm, Mmm, Mmm! And my, oh my! The ecstasy of those who ravenously crave the nourishment of being right with God! Satisfaction will be theirs!"

The highest form of well-being, the blessing of God's rule and reign, is given to those whose cravings reveal their desire to live according to their right standing with God—right in relationships, right in decision making, and right with God and others in thought, word and deed. Blessing is upon those who are amazed that the righteousness of Christ has been "credited to their account," and they crave to live righteously. They won't be disappointed; they will be satisfied.

This is another of Jesus' secrets to spiritual transformation. The Beatitudes form a spiritual growth continuum for us to monitor our progress in spiritual maturity. I learned in the first three the way to enter God's blessing. Now, the fourth beatitude assures me that I *have already* entered into a growing, personal, dynamic, vital relationship with the living God. How do I know that? My hungers and thirsts are changing. My want-to's are different. The cravings for being right with God and living right before God start rising up in me and find fulfillment in my life. Just like a child's cravings for food are a testimony to her being gloriously alive and healthy, when you start noticing cravings for righteousness in your life, it's evidence that God has come alive in you.

Too often, we don't understand the concept of righteousness. Like God's forgiveness and acceptance, we think we have to earn it. Paul's letter to the Romans is the most expansive explanation of Christ's righteousness in the Bible, and he contrasts Christ's righteousness with our inherent unrighteousness: "There is no one righteous [but God] . . . no one who seeks God . . . no one who does good" (Romans 3:10-12). And Jesus said, "There is only One who is good" (Matthew 19:17). None of us seek to live right by ourselves. We may have the fleeting notion of goodness or the ability to imagine the ideal, but when the heat is on, we don't have the power to stay true. Typically, we compromise and then rationalize.

Britney Spears was quoted about her views on having sex before marriage. You may remember she had earlier announced and always planned that she would wait until she got married for sex. But soon after she broke up with her first lover, she felt heartbroken and said, "I've only slept with one person my whole life. It was two years into my relationship with Justin, and I thought he was the one. But I was wrong! . . . The most painful thing I have ever experienced was that breakup. We were together so long and I had this vision. You think you're going to spend the rest of your life together. Where I come from, the woman is the homemaker, and that's how I was brought up—you cook for your kids. But now I realize I need my single time."[4]

Britney couldn't keep her promise to herself to remain pure. Her admission showed that she was, at least at that moment, poor in spirit. Jesus said if she admits her poverty, and instead of trying to hide the embarrassment or bury the pain, she yields her life to God, she can know the blessing of the kingdom, the highest sense of well-being on earth. And that's true for all of us.

Part of the challenge for people of affluence, fame or fortune, power or position (and by the way, compared to others in the world, everyone in America is affluent) is that our pride makes it very hard for us to admit our need. Jesus said, "It is easier for a camel to go through the eye of a needle than for someone who is rich to enter the kingdom of God" (Matthew 19:23-24). Surely the humor of Jesus' hyperbole wasn't lost on His listeners, but the truth behind it is no joke. Jesus is saying it's hard for people of means to find the kingdom of heaven. Why? Because money, fame, and power can mask our desperate need and distract us from the hurt in our hearts. And the grip of money and power is so strong that we think we can't let go.

The fourth beatitude gives evidence that you can know you have crossed over into God's kingdom and a life of blessing. How? Because you have a deep desire for setting things right. You don't want to live the old way anymore. You want to be right with God and right with people, and you have an appetite for healthy spiritual growth in righteousness. Those are sure signs of life!

How would you describe what it means to "hunger and thirst for righteousness"?

What are some specific actions people take if they live out the fourth beatitude? What are their motivations to take them?

What is God saying to you through this chapter?

CHAPTER 13

EVIDENCE OF LIFE

How can you know you've passed from death into life . . . from darkness into light? John, one of Jesus' closest disciples, writes, "No one who is born of God will continue to sin, because God's seed remains in him; he cannot go on sinning, because he has been born of God" (1 John 3:9). John certainly isn't saying that now it's impossible to sin again. He's saying that it now is impossible for someone in whom God's holy life has come alive to be happy living a lifestyle of sin. Paul wrote the Corinthians: "When someone becomes a Christian, he becomes a brand-new person inside. He is not the same anymore. A new life has begun!" (2 Corinthians 5:17 TLB)

I've celebrated my spiritual birthday for many decades. Years ago, when I was a new Christian, I was so overwhelmed with the grace of God that it created a whole new set of want-to's. I didn't want to lie anymore. I didn't want to steal. I didn't want to do drugs or use people. I didn't want to use the words that had soiled my vocabulary. Instead, I wanted to be kind. I wanted to do good. I wanted to *be* good—not to earn God's approval, but because I was already completely forgiven and had been credited with the righteousness of Christ.

I remember writing to my family to apologize for the rebellious way I had treated them. I went back to store owners I had shoplifted from, admitted my theft, and paid them for the things I'd stolen. Some of them looked at me like I was crazy. They wanted to know why I was doing this, so I told them, "Jesus has come into my life, and He wants me to live honestly." I was awakened to the value of righteous living.

Sometimes in Q & A sessions, young people will ask, "How far can I go?" The sense of the question is: "How close to the edge of sexual temptation can I walk without falling off?" That question seemed irrelevant to me in my new faith. I asked a very different question: "How close can I get to God for the rest of my life?"

I went to people I'd injured in word or deed and apologized, and I sought to make amends. I was able to help several meet Jesus. Why was I doing that? Why did it suddenly matter so much to me? Where did that hunger and thirst for putting things right come from? I had come alive, and like all living creatures, I was hungry for things that nourish, build, and strengthen. God's offer of a vibrant life in Him isn't only for a few, for those who have cleaned up their lives, for the people who have proven themselves to Him. Quite the opposite. As we've seen, the offer is for those who are humble enough to admit their need, grieve their selfishness, and want God more than anything else.

There's good news here, especially for those of us who feel like we are in some kind of race to measure up. The world tells you, "You're not pretty enough"; "You're not thin enough," "You're not smart enough," "You're not strong enough," "You're not big enough," "You're not shapely enough," "You're not rich enough," "You're not dressed well enough," "You're not popular enough," "You're not well-connected enough," and in fact, "You're just not good enough!" Jesus is telling us in these first four beatitudes that God's choice blessings of favor come to the needy, the inadequate ones, to those who feel for whatever reason they're people of the "not enough" variety.

You may be familiar with the saying, "God helps those who help themselves." Did you know that isn't in the Bible? It's found in *Poor Richard's Almanac* by Benjamin Franklin. In Jesus' view, God doesn't help those who help themselves. Instead, God helps those who *know* they need help, who *feel* they need help, who *yield* to God's help, and then receive spiritual life which cultivates their *taste* for God's help. Our hunger for living right before God doesn't come as a requirement to get to God. It comes as a gift *from* God.

How can you tell you've crossed over from death into spiritual life? You like God, you like being around people who like God, you like talking about God, and you like feeding on the truth of God. His life is giving testimony from within you that the Living Water and the Bread of Heaven are now part of your daily menu. (See John 6:32-35, 7:37-39.)

So, let me ask you: What are you hungry for? What nourishes and motivates you to get up and get going every day? What desires are driving your life? True spiritual hunger is much more than a passing curiosity or a marketing fad. It's a desire for God's reign and righteousness in your life. And when it's there, it comes with a promise from God to fill you up: you will be satisfied.

Do you shake your head and say, "That sounds great, but I'm not there yet"? You're in good company. We're all a work in progress . . . even the apostle Paul, but he assures us, "He who began a good work in you will carry it on to completion until the day of Christ Jesus" (Philippians 1:6).

What are you really hungry for? What does this hunger look like in your life? (How does it consume your thoughts, goals, daydreams, and choices?)

How does hunger for God and His purposes change everything else in our lives?

What is God saying to you through this chapter?

CHAPTER 14

THE SOURCE

Jesus' answer to the problem of sin is unique. Most people in our communities—including many in our churches—believe righteousness is "keeping the rules." And in every other world religion, righteousness is an earned commodity. The faithful are on a type of performance plan: follow the laws, adhere to the rituals, keep the rules, and you will merit a good standing. These things are done in order to measure up and secure a passing grade.

But in Jesus' view, righteousness isn't earned, it's offered. It isn't achieved, it's received, like food is received by someone who is hungry. To Jesus, true righteousness isn't self-righteousness, it's gift righteousness. It's not rule-keeping righteousness, it's grace-receiving righteousness. In his letter to the Ephesians, Paul made this crystal clear: "For it is by grace you have been saved, through faith—and this is not from yourselves, it is the gift of God—not by works, so that no one can boast" (Ephesians 2:8-9). And in writing to Titus, he told him, "But when the kindness and love of God our Savior appeared, he saved us, not because of righteous things we had done, but because of his mercy. He saved us through the washing of rebirth and renewal by the Holy Spirit" (Titus 3:4-5).

Theologians call it "imputed righteousness." This simply means that Christ transfers His own righteousness (which is beyond our ability to earn, produce, or deserve) to your account as if it were your very own. One pastor illustrates it like this, "A college student has a financial need, calls home, says, 'Mom, Dad, help! Can you impute some funds to my account?' The parents take the appropriate action to transfer money from their family bank's ample supply to their daughter or son's needy account." So it is with us and God. We cry out to Him, "I'm empty! I'm needy! I'm hungry! Help!" God responds by transferring righteousness, the perfect righteousness of His Son Jesus Christ, to our account. He fills the demand and keeps it coming.

The word translated "filled" in the fourth beatitude comes from a word that means *garden*, as in vegetable garden. When you have a vegetable garden, you don't just eat one meal. My mother-in-law has cultivated a garden that has kept her family in vegetables for years. The tummies of four different generations have been fed from her produce. Jesus was saying this is how God provides for His hungry children. He loves to satisfy the healthy appetites of His children. He just keeps the righteousness coming. Once we sit down at His table, the platter is never empty, the Server never grows tired, and His supply of grace is always sufficient. He is a filling God.

This is good news in a world system built to exploit our "constant craving," as one musical artist puts it. Many people are trying to fill the void in their lives with more and better things, but you can't fill a spiritual need with a material object. You can't satisfy the soul by pumping some substance into your body.

God the Holy Spirit is the satisfier of the soul. Somebody said, "God the Father is honey in the flower, God the Son is honey in the comb, but God the Spirit is honey in my mouth."

He is the Comforter and Counselor Jesus promised would come to His followers (John 14:16-18, 16:7). The Holy Spirit is the Spirit of Christ who has come to set up housekeeping within us.

Through the Holy Spirit, the Father draws us to Jesus (John 6:44), convicts us of our sin, makes us aware of our need for forgiveness, and brings us to Christ as Savior (John 16:7-15). The Holy Spirit regenerates our spirit and plants the seed of God's life in us (John 3:5-8). Upon your profession of faith in Christ, the Holy Spirit baptizes you into Christ (1 Corinthians 12:12-13), and by His seal, He secures you in His body forever (Ephesians 1:13-14). The Holy Spirit flows into each branch as the life-nurturing sap of the true vine Christ describes in John 15. He provides for us to live fruitful and productive lives as, by faith, we abide in Christ. We abide in Him by making His Word and prayer our dwelling place (John 15:7).

The Holy Spirit is God's unfailing battery pack. He empowers us to overcome the desires of the sinful nature within us and bear rich harvests of spiritual fruit (Galatians 5:16-25). Believers are commanded to avoid the drunkenness that comes from substance abuse, and instead, be continually "filled with the Spirit" (Ephesians 5:18). God's Spirit is our Satisfier, our Comforter and Counselor, the person of the Godhead responsible to make us thirsty and then quench our thirst, to make us hungry and then satisfy our inner appetite for God.

When do we feast at God's banquet table? Jesus encouraged His followers to make their spiritual journey a daily experience. He spoke of "daily bread" (Matthew 6:11) and the need to take up our cross "daily" (Luke 9:23). Prayer is essential. Mark's Gospel reports that, "Very early in the morning, while it was still dark, Jesus got up, left the house and went off to a solitary place, where he prayed" (1:35). All of us need a time every day that we spend reading and reflecting on the Bible and talking to God in prayer.

You wouldn't think of eating only one meal a week. Yet how many people only feed their spiritual appetites in a weekend church service? It's far healthier to have daily feedings. I like to memorize and review Bible verses that are special to me throughout the day . . . kind of like spiritual snacks or power bars. I also listen to Christian music, podcasts of sermons, and the YouVersion audio Bible when I'm on the road.

In addition to the personal feeding you can build into every day, one of the great blessings Christ brings is that every child of God is born into a family, the church. The church is a family of brothers and sisters, and we care for one another by sharing our gifts and our lives so all of God's children are built up (John 15:9-17; 1 Corinthians 12:27; Ephesians 4:11-16).

How does the feeding happen? In our church there are three arenas. First, our weekend services are where we share God's Word of hope and encouragement in the atmosphere of worship, seeking Him in Spirit and in truth. Second, we offer ministry events throughout the week for different ages and groups of people as an opportunity to dig deeper. Third, we host small groups. Some are on the weekend, some on weekdays, but each is offered as a place to grow in community by getting connected with other people who are caring for each other and learning together.

Jesus told Peter, "Do you love me? Feed my sheep" (John 21:15-17). The Lord's vision for His church is a place where people of all ages who are hungry and thirsty for new life in Christ will find it. Lambs, our newest spiritual children, are cared for as they learn to feed themselves; sheep are feeding themselves and care for each other in the flock through their involvement in each other's lives; and shepherds are raised up to share the gifts God has given them in serving those under their care.

What is the source of spiritual growth, of being fed and filled? The Spirit of God, the Word of God, and the family of God work together to provide what we need to grow strong in our faith.

What happens in the hearts, behavior, and relationships of those who trust in their goodness to earn points with God? And what happens in the people who realize the only goodness they have is because they've been clothed with Christ's righteousness?

People have different schedules. What would be a good time for you to regularly feast on God through prayer and reading the Bible?

What is God saying to you through this chapter?

CHAPTER 15

RECEIVING MERCY

"Blessed are the merciful, for they will be shown mercy."

I share God's love.

"What is the most important word in the English language?" I can still remember the day when seminary professor, Dr. Oscar Thompson, asked this question in our class. He clarified: "Outside of proper nouns and names, what is the most important word in the English language? What do you think? Any ideas?"

We volunteered a few. "Truth." "Hope." "Faith." And, of course, somebody said, "Love." Dr. Thompson's answer? "Relationship." After he let that sink in, he continued, "Relationship is the most important word in the English language." Why relationship and not love? "Well," he explained, "love is the train and relationships are the tracks love travels along. Without the tracks the train's going nowhere. Life happens in terms of relationships." Dr. Thompson challenged us, "Solve the relationship problem, and you've solved the problems of life."

I don't know if you agree with the good professor's assessment, but I'd like you to consider it as we unpack the fifth beatitude. This beatitude has "relationship" written all over it. Of course, every beatitude deals with our relationship to God, but number five marks an upward move in our spiritual growth and personal transformation that can't happen and won't happen in the absence of relationships.

If you take this beatitude out of context, rip it out of the flow of this spiritual growth continuum, and try to make it a stand-alone bumper sticker, it's not going to ring true. Does the casual observer think the highest form of well-being belongs to the merciful? I don't think so. In this world the merciful don't seem so blessed. They're often used and taken advantage of, aren't they? It's the powerful that seem to be blessed, not the merciful. Maybe mercy worked for Mother Teresa, but in my world, mercy is seen as weakness, or maybe at best, naïveté.

Sometimes well-intentioned but misguided people misinterpret Jesus on this one. Remember, it was Jesus who instructs His followers to be as "shrewd as snakes and as innocent as doves" (Matthew 10:16). That doesn't sound naïve to me. We need to grasp the context so we understand the meaning and application of this beatitude, and the context is the spiritual growth continuum of all nine. This one is right in the middle, after the first four and before the last four.

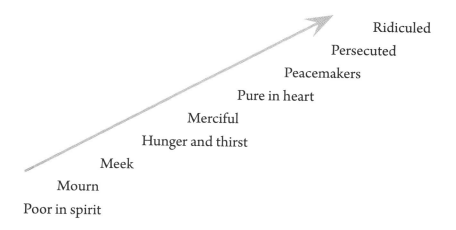

Ridiculed
Persecuted
Peacemakers
Pure in heart
Merciful
Hunger and thirst
Meek
Mourn
Poor in spirit

To recap where we've been, the first four paint pictures of our entry into the life of blessing and the foundation of transformed motives for obedience. The kingdom blessing of God comes to me as, first, I admit my need. Rationally, I admit my deficit before God. Second, I grieve my lack. Emotionally, I feel the pain and sorrow to the point that I realize something has got to change. Third, I yield my will. Volitionally, I choose to let God be my God. I humble myself under God's gracious reign, like the horse Seabiscuit under a new owner, trainer, and rider, and let Him take me where I could never go when I was trying to be my own god and run my own life.

Fourth, as a result of these three, I experience the blessing of a new *wanter*. My desires change. Beatitude four tells me I'm seized by a new hunger to live my life right with God, right in relationships, and right in decision making. I want to treat others right. I don't want to do wrong like I used to. I don't want to be held captive to sin—I want to be free. I don't want to lie, steal, cheat, or use people. I'm hungry and thirsty for my life to be right before God. And in response to the new hunger God has placed in me, He also sets the table and satisfies my longings with His loving, powerful life, showing itself in and through my life. I'm growing spiritually, and the evidence is starting to make itself known. The fruit of the Spirit is starting to bud in me: love, joy, peace, patience, kindness, goodness, faithfulness, gentleness, and self-control. So, what's the next level of spiritual growth? We move up to mercy. This one is all about relationships.

It doesn't take long to realize that when you have taken hold of Jesus' cross, there are many other hands on it with yours. You're not alone as you share the life of God. God has lots of children, and each one of us is a small part of a much larger family God is creating. Imagine a newborn, now growing to realize he or she has siblings, and the DNA of the parent is also in the brothers and sisters. Spiritually, you're in God's family, and you learn to treat your brothers and sisters as family. There are no orphans in the family of God.

Once you've experienced the evidence of God's life *in* you (beatitude four), the next level of growth is expressing God's love *through* all you say and do. Everything that has happened to this point in your development has come to you compliments of the mercy of God. The Christian understanding of mercy grows out of the Old Testament concept of *hesed,* God's "assisting faithfulness." God's mercy is His faithful assistance to us in our weakness and need.[5] In Romans 12:1 (KJV), Paul uses the phrase "mercies of God" to call his readers to a place of total surrender to God. He had just spent the previous eleven chapters explaining God's mercies—all God had done throughout redemptive history, climaxing in Jesus Christ to make salvation available to humanity. We are the grateful recipients of the wealth of God's great mercy. Now, as our tanks fill and overflow, we're ready to be merciful to others.

How would you define and describe God's mercy toward you?

Is His mercy a wonder to you? Why or why not?

What is God saying to you through this chapter?

CHAPTER 16

GIVING MERCY

Having been graced by the mercy of God in our struggle as sinners, poor and needy, we can now share the same mercy with others. And as they receive it, they'll be able to share it with still more people, so mercy multiplies. I like these descriptions:

Mercy is love in its work clothes.

Mercy is empathy in action, kindness incarnate, tender forgiveness.

Mercy is God willing to get His hands dirty to tend the garden of our lives.

When we show mercy to each other, we're loving each other God's way. We learn that none of us has the right to point the finger and say of another, "Now, there goes a real sinner. It would take a *real* miracle to change him. I'm so glad I've given God more promising material than that!" (As if it took any less a miracle of mercy to redeem each of us.) The process is familiar by now:

I share God's love.

I receive and experience God's life.

I yield my will.

I grieve my lack.

I admit my need.

This is the path we travel in our transformation toward Christlikeness. At the beatitude of mercy, Jesus doesn't just want us to *see* the many other hands holding the cross with ours; He wants us to *hold* each other's hands as we grasp the cross together. He wants us to show mercy—God's faithful assistance—to one another, in the same way we have received it from Him. We are to follow His example and take the initiative, offering it to one another and experiencing together the power of divine community.

The church of Jesus Christ is to be a family of friends, a community of mercy, where the truth is spoken in love and people grow in grace. It should be a place where the "one anothers" of the New Testament are practiced regularly: "serve one another," "be kind to one another," "bear one another's burdens," and "pray for one another," to mention just a few. (There are about fifty of them in the New Testament.) The church is the place where mercy is lavished on one and all, and the royal character of our King sets the tone for the entire kingdom community. In this family, instead of demanding our "rights" or insisting on "what's fair," we learn to treat each other the way God has treated us—with exquisite mercy.

Shakespeare described it this way: "The quality of mercy is not strained, it drops as the gentle rain from heaven upon the place beneath: it is twice blessed; it blesses him that gives and him that takes; 'tis mightiest in the mightiest; it becomes the throned monarch better than his crown; . . . it is an attribute to God himself, and earthly power doth then show likest God's when mercy seasons justice."[6]

When we treat each other the way our King has treated us, we're learning to live as royalty, and we're growing spiritually. Surely this is what Jesus had in mind when He told His disciples: "As I have loved you, so you must love one another. By this everyone will know that you are my disciples, if you love one another" (John 13:34-35).

Think of His audience. They weren't exactly all-stars! There was impetuous, foot-in-his-mouth Peter and thoughtful, reflective Nathanael. There was Matthew, a former tax collector for the Romans, and Simon the Zealot, whose political loyalties were devoted to the overthrow of Rome. There were the Sons of Thunder, James and John, ready to call fire down from the sky and burn up a village resistant to Jesus' coming, as well as Thomas the doubter. And Jesus tells them, "You guys have got to love one another—not superficially, not gritting your teeth, but with hearts overflowing with love, kindness, and mercy. In fact, I want you to love each other *in the same way* I have loved you. This is how the world will know you're My followers." Jesus knew that when that kind of diversity of opinion, personality, background, and perspective form a community that cares, the world notices.

We think we have seating and parking problems in our churches now. If word got out that people are being loved the way Jesus loves, that mercy is flowing from heaven and building a community that cares through the lives of people yielded to God—needy and grieving, yes, but full of His life and now sharing love from the heart—people in our cities and towns would beat the doors down to get some of that!

Biblical community is one of the core values of every church, but a picture is worth so much more than words. A quilt represents the diversity and beauty of a Christ-centered community. It can be made from scraps, with all kinds of colors and designs, but scraps nonetheless. And with a skillful hand, the artist crafts them together—individuality and diversity turned into a thing of beauty.

A quilt is a picture of the church, formed from the pieces of our lives, taken out of the scrap heap of our isolation and alienation. In our church, we have people from over fifty countries who speak more than twenty-nine different languages and represent every ZIP code in our county. God takes the needle of grace and the thread of mercy to weave our lives together into His kingdom quilt.

Community has the power to do many things. It draws us close so we feel that we belong. When I was a kid, I remember using a big quilt at our house to make a fort. There was room in that fort for me, my brother, and my sister, and when we could get them to squeeze down there and join us, there was even room enough for Mother and Daddy. We had room for the whole family under that quilt.

In every church, the metaphor of a quilt reminds us that there's room enough for all of God's children in church fellowship. We have the power to say, "You belong. You matter to us. We have a place for you." This is the power of acceptance, forgiveness, and validation.

A quilt also represents the power of nurture. I've always loved the feel of the cloth around my neck. I don't know why. Maybe it reminds me of the times in my childhood when my mother would offer me her tender loving care to nurse me back to health. If I had a chest cold, she would rub the Vicks VapoRub on my chest and neck, then wrap a warm soft cloth around my neck. She would pull the covers up real snug as she tucked me into bed. I still like to sleep with the covers pulled up around my neck.

The power of community is the power to nurture, comfort, encourage, and share tender loving care. Community starts with each person's experience of God's mercy, is deepened as mercy is faithfully expressed, and is multiplied into the lives of others in our families, our neighborhoods, and our towns and cities.

Mercy is the glue of our spiritual relationships.

Who has shown mercy toward you? What difference did (or does) it make?

Why is a quilt a good metaphor for biblical community?

What is God saying to you through this chapter?

CHAPTER 17

UNLEASHING MERCY

The power of community is found in our ability to envision and unleash our full redemptive potential in the kingdom of God. Community is where we find the freedom to become all that God has gifted us to be. Community forms the wings of mercy that catch the wind of God's Spirit and lift us to the heights.

And as you give mercy, more mercy grows. Jesus said, "Blessed are the merciful, for they will be shown mercy." Peter knew this about the ministry of mercy from his personal experience with Jesus and the disciples. It's probably why he later would write: "Above all, love each other deeply, because love covers over a multitude of sins" (1 Peter 4:8).

I like that: love *covers*. This sounds like something a quilt would do. Love offers acceptance and forgiveness. C.S. Lewis once said, "Everyone says forgiveness is a lovely idea, until they have something to forgive."[7] Isn't this true? When wounded or slighted, I find it much more natural to take offense, hold a grudge, and nurse resentment instead of offering forgiveness. It just doesn't feel fair. We conclude: "After what they've done, they don't deserve to be forgiven!" But here's the truth: the only time forgiveness can be offered is when the offending party doesn't deserve it. That's when God offers it. F.D. Bruner says, "The first test of obedience in Jesus' ethic is not whether obedience makes one morally tougher, but whether it makes one more humanly tenderer—merciful."[8] In other words, if you really want to know if you have experienced the forgiveness of God, see what kind of forgiver you are. Check your mercy quotient. In the fellowship of the forgiven, we rub shoulders and bump into fellow sinners who are also under the quilt of God's mercy—and that's where we learn how to practice forgiveness.

Jesus is saying, "In My kingdom, those who are full of mercy are powerful people. They aren't marginalized or minimized. They're the mainstream currents in the river of healing love." When injury and offense come, we turn to the strong medicine of mercy, which, when applied, brings healing to everyone it touches: the injured, the offender, and the associated parties. And it's Jesus' response to injury, bigotry, and hate.

Jesus says, "I desire mercy, not sacrifice" (Matthew 9:13). What did He mean? As you know, there is a kind of piety, a show of religious righteousness, a pride in our sacrifice of money, time, and effort, that hardens hearts. It makes you more severe with others as you become more strict and severe with yourself. Jesus was constantly confronting the prideful abuses of the Pharisees. (See Matthew 9:9-13 and 12:1-14.) The fifth beatitude counters the hardness that self-righteousness brings. It claims, "The first evidence of God's righteousness filling your life (beatitude four) is the presence and practice of mercy with fellow sinners (beatitude five)."

Peter instructs us, "Offer hospitality to one another without grumbling." We are to make room in our homes and hearts. Just like I made room in my fort under the quilt, we offer each other heavenly hospitality, with room enough for all those forgiven by God. Peter continues, "Each of you should use whatever gift you have received to serve others, as faithful stewards of God's grace in its various forms" (1 Peter 4:9-10).

Finally, the church is to be a place where hope for the future is envisioned and people are unleashed to become all God intends them to be. Forgiven of sin, embraced by the family, and empowered by God's mercy, we grow together into the family tree of God's kingdom.

It's easy for people to come and go in churches and not make any significant connections with others. For this reason, it's important to participate in a small group where we encourage and challenge each other to grow in our faith. All of us need this level of spiritual relationships. Nobody is perfect, but here, all of us are receiving and giving mercy as we learn, pray, care, serve, and reach out to become more like Jesus.

The redwood is the tallest of trees, growing to a height of almost 400 feet. That's forty stories high! You would think that they must have very deep roots, but they don't. Actually, they have shallow root systems so they can gather all the surface moisture. But their roots spread out in all directions and intertwine with those of the surrounding trees. They're locked together in such a way that when storm winds blow, the trees strengthen and sustain each other. This is why you almost never see a redwood standing alone. At that height, they need each other to survive.

It's the same with people. God has designed us that as we grow, ascending the heights toward heaven and facing the storms of life, we find strength in standing together and sharing the roots of God's mercy. As we grow taller in Christ, we intertwine relationally at the ground level of vulnerability and deep encouragement.

This is one of the secrets of spiritual transformation: we share God's love in a caring, merciful community. This isn't a new idea. Paul told the believers in Colossae, "Just as you trusted Christ to save you, trust him, too, for each day's problems; live in vital union with him. Let your roots grow down into him and draw up nourishment from him. See that you go on growing in the Lord, and become strong and vigorous in the truth you were taught. Let your lives overflow with joy and thanksgiving for all he has done" (Colossians 2:6-7 TLB).

Is your life overflowing in this way?

In what way is God's mercy a powerful medicine?

How is mercy also the most effective fertilizer for spiritual growth?

What is God saying to you through this chapter?

CHAPTER 18

MORE THAN SKIN DEEP

"Blessed are the pure in heart, for they shall see God."

I see God's light.

Late one night we were driving down the interstate in Missouri from Springfield to Branson when the car began missing, sputtering, and losing power. Finally, it died. I started it and we drove for a while, but it died again. It was a problem with the fuel system—probably bad gas from the station where we had filled up less than a half hour before. After a few miles of on-again, off-again sputtering down the highway, we finally coasted down an exit into a gas station.

I'm sure it was quite a sight: there I was in the middle of the night, my family locked inside our stalled car, and I'm squatting beside it with a hose in my mouth, doing the siphon dance like a snake charmer, trying to get the bad gas out so I could put fresh, clean fuel in. The moral of the story? Impurities in your system can leave you going nowhere . . . with a bad taste in your mouth . . . and smelling like you need a match put to you. One of the things my wife Lisa remembers about that experience is me belching gas fumes all the way home! (I must admit, I've never quite mastered that whole siphoning thing.)

We later discovered that not only were there impurities in our fuel, but the fuel filter was clogged and had to be replaced. I'm here to testify: Pure fuel and clean filters make for happier travelers . . . as do honest mechanics.

In the sixth beatitude, Jesus explains a similar benefit for spiritual travelers: "Blessed are the pure in heart, for they will see God." According to Jesus, happiness in life's journey flows from a system free from contamination and transports you into the field of divine vision. This is a fascinating concept. Jesus is saying that the greatest benefit of life—beholding God—comes from purity in the human heart and clarity of focus. The heart is the control tower of your soul, mission central to who you are and what you do. Imagine 100 percent clarity and purity at your core. Jesus says it can happen.

Though popular culture continues to try to erode the value of sexual purity, it's ironic how many other fields extol the benefits of purity. Pure water is big business these days, and there are a dozen varieties of bottled water at every grocery store. We like our water pure and free from pollutants, don't we? The value of gold is directly related to its level of purity, and people speak of "24-carat pure gold." Many of us have virus-blocking software on our computers to protect us from downloading contaminated information or some clandestine and destructive virus that ruins our files. When a loved one needs a blood transfusion, we want the supply to be nothing less than pure. Why? Because we understand the value of purity in our blood. If you're dining out and you find a hair in your salad or a food smudge inside your drinking glass, what do you do? You ask for another to avoid the contamination of impurities. Many people prefer natural foods because they want to avoid chemical additives and artificial preservatives. In all of these areas, purity brings many benefits.

Jesus states that purity in the spiritual realm is even more important than it is in the physical realm. It is both preferable and possible to experience purity, to be clean and clear, in the deepest part of who you are—free from contamination and pollutants, clear of spot, stain, and blemish. And the result? You will see God . . . with wide-eyed wonderment in remarkable new ways, no doubt.

We need to remember that Jesus' way to purity was very different from what people believed. It's not strict external adherence to a religious system of moral behavior. The religious leaders of His day believed the true test of spiritual fitness was found in how many of their rules were kept. The more rules you keep, the higher your score with God. Jesus courageously exposed the hypocrisy of any religion that focuses on the outside of a person's appearance while neglecting the person's inner soul and real spiritual condition. His most scathing remarks were reserved for these religious leaders. Jesus didn't beat around the bush when He told them:

> "Woe to you, teachers of the law and Pharisees, you hypocrites! You clean the outside of the cup and dish, but inside they are full of greed and self-indulgence. Blind Pharisee! First clean the inside of the cup and dish, and then the outside also will be clean. Woe to you, teachers of the law and Pharisees, you hypocrites! You are like whitewashed tombs, which look beautiful on the outside but on the inside are full of dead men's bones and everything unclean. In the same way, on the outside you appear to people as righteous but on the inside you are full of hypocrisy and wickedness." (Matthew 23:25-28)

Extreme Makeover was a reality television show that aired from 2002 to 2007. In each program, the audience tracks the external transformation of someone who has been selected as the lucky recipient of a complete change in their outward appearance. Through plastic surgery their face is shifted and lifted—along with various other body parts. Their teeth are straightened and whitened. Their hair is styled by a professional, and their wardrobe is selected by the finest specialists in the colors and styles that flatter the recipient's new body type. Following each extreme makeover, the person is transported by limousine to the place of their coming out where anxious loved ones await the unveiling.

The few times I've seen the show, the changes in the appearance of the individual are nothing less than dramatic. When each candidate is presented, there are tears, screams, gasps, laughter, and exclamations of disbelief. It's not unusual to hear the recipient say something like, "It's still me! I'm still in here."

But as I watch, I wonder what the future holds for the people and their families down the road. Maybe there should be a follow-up show called "More than Skin Deep" to explore the issues that weren't resolved by cosmetic surgery and the new ones that were brought to the surface (pun intended) in the process.

Jesus wants to conduct an extreme makeover in our lives, but it's one that goes all the way to the heart. Are you ready? Are you willing? Are you eager?

What are some differences between being spiritually pure and legalistically rigid?

Is the kind of purity in this beatitude attractive to you? Why or why not?

What is God saying to you through this chapter?

CHAPTER 19

ALL THE WAY DOWN

Here's how Jesus gets extreme: Though our focus is usually on outer characteristics, Jesus insists that God looks at the heart. Since the source of our problem is the heart, the solution must focus there, too. Jesus explained, "What comes out of a person is what defiles them. For it is from within, out of a person's heart, that evil thoughts come—sexual immorality, theft, murder, adultery, greed, malice, deceit, lewdness, envy, slander, arrogance and folly. All these evils come from inside and defile a person" (Mark 7:20-23).

The Pharisees had a strict plan that gave them the appearance of righteousness and purity through external rule-keeping. Jesus counters this approach by saying, in essence, "You can't cure cancer with cosmetic surgery. It takes more than a coat of paint to save a house with termites. And I've got a solution: Purity all the way down . . . a growing transformation in the heart . . . a process in which contaminants and pollutants are being purged and replaced at the heart level. This is the acid test of spiritual authenticity."

"Blessed are the pure in heart." According to Jesus, it's about internals, not externals. Here's where Dr. Jesus gets extreme: He's reminding us that God sees right through the pretense and masquerade of our external hypocrisies and goes right for the heart of what really drives us. What is the real motive of what we do? This beatitude makes us ask questions we'd rather avoid—the probing kind we tend to deflect by listing our performance of external rules. We say, "I'm in church, aren't I? That counts for something. I have a Bible. I've been baptized. I put ten bucks in the plate. I'm covered. Get off my back!" This beatitude is a CAT scan that calls us to examine why we do what we do . . . and what is going on inside us as we do it. Everything is exposed: our hopes and fears in our most important relationships, our honesty at work, and even our secret thoughts. What is really at the center of our motivations? Are we clean and clear at the center?

I'm not just pointing my finger at you. Jesus looks at me and says, "Bill, you have to deal with these questions too, and not because you're a pastor, but because you're one of My children. These are heart questions, and they are what matter most to Me. When your heart is clean and clear, then you will see Me at work in your world." This is Jesus' promise: purity leads to perspective. Hebrews 12:14 says that "without holiness no one will see the Lord." Jesus is promising the experience of God's holiness in the deepest parts of the soul and spirit—and then, as a result, the ability to see God at work in and around us.

Since coming to South Florida, I've found a new sport: free-dive fishing with a Hawaiian sling. I'll gear up with my snorkel, mask, fins, and weight belt, and then, taking my sling in hand, head off into the ocean with a few friends to see what catch awaits me. I'm not talking scuba. We don't use tanks. This is strictly hold-your-breath-and-swim-underwater fishing.

One piece of equipment that I absolutely can't do without is my dive mask. Without my mask, I can't see a thing underwater. My vision is fuzzy and the salt water hurts my eyes. But with the help of my mask, a field of vision is created and I'm able to literally see underwater. Through the mask, I've been introduced to a whole new world of beauty and wonder under the sea.

In beatitude number six, Jesus speaks about how each of us acquires the ability to see into the spiritual dimension—beyond the fuzzy, sometimes painful, smoke-gets-in-your-eyes distractions of this world and into the serene beauty of God's holiness and transcendent glory. Purity of heart is like the clarity of the lens in my dive mask, only instead of seeing fish, mollusks, and reefs, purity of heart helps me see God. The Bible says that God is invisible (1 Timothy 1:17), so this promise sounds ridiculous, doesn't it? How can anyone *see* God? But this is the point. We have been learning about authentic spiritual transformation: how a human being, created in the image of God, wired for relationship with God, but separated from God by sin and its consequences, can be redeemed. Redemption is more than a ticket to heaven. It's being released from our fallenness and depravity and completely reconciled to God, learning to live in the fullness of His blessing until Jesus returns or we die and inherit our heavenly home.

Jesus is taking us to another level in our spiritual maturity, our personal transformation, and He says there's a way we can live that will open our eyes to God's activity in the world. In John 5:19 Jesus says, "Very truly I tell you, the Son can do nothing by himself; he can do only what he sees his Father doing, because whatever the Father does the Son also does." How did Jesus live His life? By doing whatever He *sees* His Father doing. How can you know you're growing spiritually? Your eyes are opened to see God at work. You come to a place where you can say to God, "I have eyes for You!" You *see* Him showing up in your life, in your relationships, and in your world.

How do you see the invisible? The same way you hear the inaudible and the same way you feel the intangible—by grace through faith. God works the miracle of salvation in your life. Remember the process. This isn't a stand-alone beatitude. It's part of a whole, another level in a spiritual continuum of growth. We come into the kingdom by grace through faith, and we grow in the kingdom by grace through faith.

As growth is taking place, God works in my heart in a way that clarifies the viewscreen of my life and the way I see Him—to the point I can honestly say, "I see God's light." This is the blessing for the pure in heart. The highest kind of well-being for us is being changed by God, moving upward along the transformation continuum.

You may be saying to yourself, *I'm not so sure I've had too many God sightings lately!* Check your progress on the continuum. Start at the beginning and ask yourself, *Have I admitted to God and myself that I absolutely need Him? Have I turned from my pride and yielded my will to Him in honest surrender? Do my want-to's reflect a hunger for a life right with God and right with others? How about my relationships in the fellowship? Am I learning to love people who aren't like me but are just as loved by God? Or am I tempted to think my sins were probably easier for God to forgive than theirs?*

Please don't get confused. Self-righteousness loves to play dress-up as Christianity. Run away from that as fast as you can! Jesus predicted a very rude awakening coming for all who depend on any form of self-salvation to take them into the presence of holy God.

What are we to gather from this? First, that legalistic, self-serving moralism will, in the final analysis, fail you completely. Keeping rules and pursuing morality in your own strength is not the key to holiness in the heart. And second, if we're not seeing God at work in our lives, it's a strong indicator we aren't going to see God when our lives are over. This is hard to hear, but as we're learning, the Beatitudes aren't Jesus' version of self-help to a happier life. Jesus offers happiness, joy, peace, and blessing beyond what this world can give—and only He can give it. Purity and holiness must be received as a gift from the hand of a gracious, wise, and holy God. And when we receive it, it goes all the way down.

What are some reasons it's so easy to let "self-righteousness play dress-up Christianity"?

What do you think it means to "see God" in your faith journey?

What is God saying to you through this chapter?

CHAPTER 20

TRANSFORMED BY WORSHIP

How can we know we're growing in purity and holiness? When we're seeing more and more of God at work in our lives and in our world. How does it happen? One way is in and through worship. In Isaiah 6, the prophet is worshiping in the temple when he sees the Lord high and lifted up. In the light of God's awesome holiness, the young prophet is made aware of the impurities in his life. He is cleansed by God's atoning fire of forgiveness, and then God gives him a mission. All of this happened through an encounter with God through worship. Worship is the means by which our heart's affection and our mind's attention find their focus in giving God His rightful priority in our lives; it is profound reverence for a sovereign God, holy, high and lifted up. Worship functions like my dive mask; it helps me clarify my focus so I can see God.

One of the ways we define worship at our church is prioritizing God. We know we're worshiping when we're giving God His rightful throne in our lives. When we worship rightly, we cut through the fog, the fuzziness, the pain and distractions, and we envision God in the splendor of His holiness. We prioritize God over everything and everyone else. We give Him our heart's primary affection and our mind's priority attention.

When we worship, we return to our first love. In his first letter, John reminds us of the starting point: "We love because he first loved us" (1 John 4:19). We offer ourselves to God all day every day, always in response to His love, grace, and mercy. Paul reminds us, "Therefore, I urge you, brothers and sisters, in view of God's mercy, to offer your bodies as a living sacrifice, holy and pleasing to God—this is your true and proper worship" (Romans 12:1). In worship, we set our minds on the things of God. Paul wrote, "Set your hearts on things above, where Christ is, seated at the right hand of God. Set your minds on things above, not on earthly things" (Colossians 3:1). Worship involves the focus of our thoughts, the devotion of our hearts, and the offering of everything in our hands to God. Then, freed from distractions, our hearts seek God and find Him. In the same way prescription glasses help us see, worship helps us find our focus as our hearts are changed by His grace and truth.

Worship isn't a matter of forms or styles—they come and go over the years. We can see a long and varied history from the earliest house churches in the first centuries through the times of persecution when worship was done in silent catacombs, from the Middle Ages with the formalism of the cathedrals to the Reformation when the Word of God was again put in the language and music of the people, from the last 200 years in liturgy and hymnody to the new reformation of contemporary worship. Forms and venues are like the wineskins that adapt to accommodate the new wine of the Spirit, but beatitude six speaks to the heart of worship—to what's going on in your heart and mind as you focus on God, and the blessing that comes to those whose hearts are growing in purity.

The word *pure* has three basic definitions in the Bible. First, physically, it means being purified by fire, such as burning away the dross in gold, and it means "cleaned," like a vine is pruned so it bears more fruit. Second, in a Levitical sense, it refers to the priests avoiding ceremonial uncleanness. Third, ethically, it refers to being free from corrupt desire, from sin and guilt, from any touch of duplicity, hypocrisy or guile. It means real, sincere, genuine, blameless, unstained devotion to God.

How can we experience this level of purity? Through the process of spiritual growth. We receive the work of Christ by the grace of God through faith, and He sanctifies us. We can't purify ourselves, but we can set ourselves—heart, mind, and will—on Him, and welcome His cleansing work just like Isaiah when the angel brought the fire from the altar and touched his lips to remove his sin. In worship we can welcome the work of God that changes our hearts.

How do we do that? The way you got in is the way you go on: Admit your need by faith, grieve your lack by faith, and yield your will by faith. We pray as Jesus taught us, "Thy kingdom come," which means "My kingdom goes!" Then we receive God's life by faith, we share God's love by faith, and we pursue God's light by faith. That's how we grow from being poor in spirit to pure in heart.

Let me offer ten practical ways to maximize your worship experience.

1. Buy a Bible you can understand. *The Message* version, translated by Eugene Peterson, is easy to read. The study Bible I use and recommend is the New International Version of the *Life Application Study Bible.*

2. Set a daily time to read, pray, and worship. Don't wait until the weekend. Reading God's Word, listening to praise and worship music, and having conversations with the Lord every day will strengthen your weekend worship.

3. Get involved in a group that prays and worships together. Jesus had a group, and you need one, too. Get connected to a small group of people so you can share God's life, love, and light.

4. Select a weekend service that speaks your heart language, and attend every week. Many churches offer a choice of worship formats, so find one that fits and make it your holy habit to be there every seven days.

5. Arrive in time to be parked and seated before the service begins. Here's a novel idea: Get in the habit of being early. In our culture, if you aren't intentional, it won't happen. Church services are packed with opportunities to experience God and His truth. Don't miss a single minute.

6. Free yourself of distractions. When you sit down, turn off your cell phone, and let your preschoolers enjoy the children's program. You, and all those around you, will be glad you did. (And your little ones will be happier in an environment designed especially for them.)

7. Pray over the elements of the service you are about to experience. Preview the order of worship and ask God to use every part to speak to someone's heart—especially yours. Pray for every person who will be leading from the platform, and pray for the ones who will be worshiping on your left and right.

8. Be kind in making room for others as they arrive. Extend the quilt of community to those around you. Make room for others who didn't arrive early or who had trouble finding a parking space. Remember, your church is only as friendly as you are!

9. Seek God with your heart, mind, and body in the service. Sing the songs. Pray along with the prayers. Listen and learn during artistic presentations and during the teaching. Respond as God leads. Give of yourself in the offering. Throw your heart into the

service. Jesus said, "Seek and you will find" (Matthew 7:7). Offer God your mind's attention, your heart's affection, and your life's devotion, and expect God to reveal himself to you.

10. Ask God to show you ways to apply and share what you've received. Pray something like this: "How may I serve, Lord? Enable me to make a difference in my world. Show me how to apply the truth I've heard and bring glory to You in everything I say and do."

Isn't that what Jesus said really matters? "God is spirit, and his worshipers must worship in the Spirit and in truth" (John 4:24).

Describe a season in your life when worship has been particularly meaningful to you.

Which of the practical suggestions do you want to apply? What difference will it (or they) make?

What is God saying to you through this chapter?

KINGDOM ADVENTURE

"Blessed are the peacemakers,

for they will be called children of God.

Blessed are those who are persecuted because of

righteousness,

for theirs is the kingdom of heaven."

(Matthew 5:9-10)

CHAPTER 21

UP FOR A CHALLENGE

*"Blessed are the peacemakers,
for they will be called children of God."*

I join God's work.

I like to think I'm always up for a challenge. I love adventure . . .
living life on the edge. One recent challenge took me to the very edge,
but it came with an opportunity to do some good. The local chapter
of Youth for Christ challenged pastors to go "over the edge" by rappelling down a ten-story building. It was a fundraiser to help at-risk
teens, and I saw a need that compelled me to get involved: youth violence. Natasha, one of the YFC volunteer staff members, challenged
me to go over the edge. I said, "I'm in!"

Before I did it, I asked everybody to pray for me. My wife Lisa
and I love Youth for Christ, and members of our church have served
on their board through the years. I made the commitment to hang
on a rope 100 feet above the sidewalk. Did I mention that I don't like
heights? More to the point, I'm terrified of heights! Just thinking of it
makes my palms sweaty. But I needed to face down my fears. I wasn't
participating just for the fun of it. I was doing it for Natasha and the
kids they reach.

Not long before the event, our local news carried a story about a
high school girl who was shot at a bus stop by her boyfriend. That's

the community where Natasha follows Jesus. It's one of many neigh-borhoods where people are dying, lives are hanging in the balance, families are on the brink, and eternity is at stake. And Jesus can make the difference.

But He does it through His people—through Natasha and the rest of us who have the compassion and courage to get involved. This is Jesus' plan: to change *you* through His blessing, and then change the *world* through you. That's the great Kingdom Adventure. Jesus' point in this beatitude is that peacemakers are willing to go "over the edge," reach beyond their normal limits, and get out of their comfort zones to bring God's love and strength to people in conflict.

Let's stop to briefly review the continuum of growth in the Beatitudes: The first three speak of Kingdom *Access*—how to begin the journey and experience the blessing of life-change salvation that comes when you see your need, feel your need, and yield your need to God, making Christ your Savior and King. Next we're introduced to our Kingdom *Affluence*, appropriating the resources God provides for our journey in Christ: your family blessings of fullness, forgiveness, and focus. And now, in Jesus' next two beatitudes, we're brought into the Kingdom *Adventure*: "Blessed are the peacemakers for they will be called the children of God. Blessed are those who are persecuted be-cause of righteousness, for theirs is the kingdom of heaven" (Matthew 5:9-10). What does this mean? We're bringing heaven to earth—up there to down here right now. We could summarize these two like this: Making peace and facing pressure are part of the blessing in the Kingdom Adventure.

God has a two-part plan for you and this world. It involves, first, making peace, sharing healing and wholeness in this world, and sec-ond, facing pressure, responding to resistance and opposition. Diane Long, NFL wife to Howie and mom to Chris (both now Super Bowl champs), was asked, "How have you dealt with the pressure?" She re-sponded, "Pressure is a privilege."

Jesus says that as you follow Him in the pathway of blessing, you are going to know the same privilege. You will be taken to the edge of your seat in excitement and thrilled to discover how God uses you to be part of His solution in a lost and broken world. That's what true children of God do. But let me warn you: This adventure will demand a lot from you. You'll be taken to the end of yourself, challenged to acquire more wisdom than you've ever known, more love for difficult people than you've ever experienced, and more tenacity than you've ever shown. Are you ready for all that? If you've moved through the spiritual growth process up to this point, you're ready.

Where do we make peace? In families, at work, in neighborhoods, in our communities, and in the wider world as we see people suffering under oppression and in conflict with one another. Do you see any suffering and conflict in your world? Of course you do. We all do. Now, what are you going to do about it?

What are some relationships around you that need you to step in and make peace?

What's your plan to get involved? What are the limitations and risks?

What is God saying to you through this chapter?

CHAPTER 22

PEACE OR PIECES?

What do the following things have in common: The Heisman Trophy, Mount Everest, the Fortune 100, the Pulitzer Prize, the Nobel Peace Prize, the World Series Championship? They all represent the apex, the summit, the zenith in their respective fields. They represent the high end of performance and achievement. In the same way, the final beatitudes listed in Matthew 5 represent the high end of transformational living for the Christ-follower.

In this pursuit, we need encouragement. We need to know that Jesus is our leader, our shepherd, and our commander. Every would-be, high-end beatitude Christ-follower should commit this verse to memory: "I have told you these things, so that in me you may have peace. In this world you will have trouble. But take heart! I have overcome the world" (John16:33).

Of course, you know what tribulation is. It's lots and lots of trouble. Jesus came to a world in trouble to offer peace—in fact, to make peace between us and God when we were His enemies. The Bible says when Jesus went to the cross, He was delivered to death for our sins and raised to life for our justification. And "Therefore," according to Romans 5:1 "since we have been justified through faith, we have peace with God through our Lord Jesus Christ."

Apart from Christ we're lost in sin, condemned beyond our ability to remedy our plight before God. Along with us, our world, across the tailspin of human history, has spiraled in a state of trouble and tribulation. But Christ in love has "regarded my lowly estate and has shed His own blood for my soul."[9]

As I begin to comprehend this, and I respond to it in faith, God's redemption is made real in my life. My life begins to change, and the Beatitudes show me the process. Look again at the lengthening continuum:

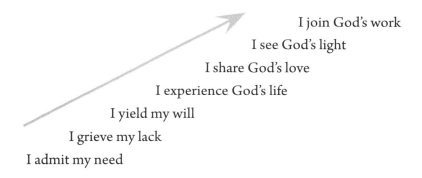

I join God's work
I see God's light
I share God's love
I experience God's life
I yield my will
I grieve my lack
I admit my need

As we follow Jesus and gradually grow to be more like Him, it should come as no surprise that He provides a way for us to see God at work in this world, and He has called us to join Him in His work. This is what beatitude seven is all about: the life of blessing is experiencing the highest well-being possible for a human to know. Each consecutive beatitude introduces us to another level in the continuum of spiritual growth and personal transformation. Number seven calls us to join God in His work.

What is a peacemaker? One who takes the initiative to be righteously redemptive in the middle of hatred, abandonment, and conflict. This is the first blessing in which the outcome is our being called "children of God." We're recognized as family members of the divine and siblings of Jesus. And the family resemblance is striking. Why? Because we're behaving the same way He would to enact God's great redemptive work of making peace—being a minister of the gospel to a divided and hurting world. We're Christ's ambassadors, ministers of reconciliation in a world torn by strife. We courageously enter into the fray and are part of the solution to the problem.

The movie *Saving Private Ryan* presents a powerful illustration of this truth. The story tracks an Army Ranger unit under the command of Captain John Miller, who, upon surviving the successful but costly D-Day invasion of Omaha Beach, is assigned to lead a squad to rescue the last surviving son in a family of four soldier brothers, Private James Francis Ryan. The Rangers go behind enemy lines, in harm's way, fulfilling their orders at great personal sacrifice—the shedding of blood and the loss of life. Others died that Ryan might live, that one child might be reunited with his mother and a relationship be restored and preserved. Miller and his squad go deep into enemy territory to seek and to save that which was lost.

Does the story line sound familiar? Those are the words of Jesus: "For the Son of Man came to seek and to save the lost" (Luke 19:10). Where do we find the lost? Everywhere we look. Jesus said, "Follow me and I will make you fishers of men" (Matthew 4:19 KJV). He will build into His followers the heart, muscle, and soul that will put us in touch with human need at every level and use us to help rescue people in need.

This part of spiritual growth introduces us to high-end beatitude living. Think of it like this: In the first three beatitudes, we pass through the entryway of the household of faith and are continually reminded of God's great grace. Next, we're brought to the dining room table where we hunger and thirst for righteousness. This is the "Feed me," stage of Christian growth. In beatitude five we then move to the family room, where we share the mercy quilt of encouragement and empowerment among the family of God. Beatitude six ushers us into the family altar of worship, where we have the eyes of our hearts opened to God's work. And then, beatitude seven turns our eyes and hearts to a world in need, a field white for harvest, where we join Jesus in His great work of redemption, of search and rescue, where God's peace—the *shalom*, the blessing of wholeness—is shared with others who are in need in our marketplaces, neighborhoods, schools, and mission fields.

Here, our focus isn't only on those within the body but to those who are on the outside, to those who are far from God, who have lost their faith, who are struggling but would respond if someone reached out to them. In Matthew 25 Jesus said that those who belong to God actively provide for people in need by feeding the hungry, clothing the naked, befriending the lonely, taking care of the sick, and visiting those in prison. In the Great Commission, Jesus challenged His followers to take the good news of the kingdom to all people everywhere—every language and every ethnic group in every corner of the world. Don't leave anybody out! We're God's partners in His redemptive purpose.

Jesus wants us to share with others the life, love, and light we have received from Him. As we do, tangible needs are met and people experience God's life-changing grace. The ones doing the ministry also grow in ways that simply wouldn't happen any other way. You and I will never grow to be like Jesus unless we regularly and wisely reach out to people . . . that is, unless we're involved in sharing the grace we've found in Christ with others in ways they can understand. Many churches provide outreach opportunities, but don't wait for a project. Start sharing with the people in your world. Watch God work, and watch yourself grow.

Why are we here? Why does God leave us on earth after we're saved? To share the blessing of the gospel of peace.

Jesus said, "As the Father has sent me, I am sending you" (John 20:21). Where, how, when, and to whom is He sending you?

What are your concerns about interacting with people about Jesus? What's your plan? Who can help you?

What is God saying to you through this chapter?

CHAPTER 23

DIVE IN AND MAKE A DIFFERENCE

Making peace and facing pressure are part of the blessing in the Kingdom Adventure. The Christmas angels told the shepherds, "Glory to God in the highest, and on earth peace, good will toward men" (Luke 2:14 KJV), and they spread that word wherever they went. That's how the peace of God, His wholeness and healing, gets to the neighborhoods of our world—through His people. They *take* it there and *make* it there.

What does that have to do with you? If you're a seeker, checking out the faith, I'm talking about your future. If you're a believer, your name is all over this. If you want to make a difference and have an impact, Jesus has you in mind. If you have ever seen a problem and thought, *Somebody should* do *something*, if you've ever wished for a hero to sweep in and come to the rescue, this is God's invitation and challenge to get up and get going. When God puts a need on your heart, He's saying, "I can use you to do that!"—maybe not in the way someone else might do it, but in a way that fits your gifts and is no less effective.

That's what *this* part of the pathway of blessing is about: the adventure of joining God in His work in our world. We pursue justice, love mercy, and persevere under pressure, not *giving* up but *standing* up to wage peace and righteousness in all arenas of life. People in our world need peace, and God wants to use you to share it. As you join His work, you become part of the great adventure.

In the early 90's, Steven Curtis Chapman wrote a song with this chorus:

> Saddle up your horses
> We've got a trail to blaze.
> Through the wild blue yonder of God's Amazing Grace.
> Let's follow our leader into the Glorious unknown.
> This is a life like no other
> This is the great adventure.[10]

I want to ask people of every age, from adolescents to those who don't want to tell people how old they are: Are you finding your edge in God's kingdom? Jesus' church is here to help you with that. Our pathway to blessing helps you identify your gifts and put them into service, first connecting in a group and caring for others there, and then in volunteer ministry. Grow beyond yourself by helping others in the church. As Paul says in Ephesians 4:3, "Make every effort to keep the unity of the Spirit through the bond of peace." That's peace-making right in your local church.

But it doesn't stop there. God moves us beyond church walls into our communities. Take a moment right now and reflect on where God has placed you. Ask God's blessing for your neighborhood, your home, your workplace, or your school. Where you live, love. Where you live, serve. If you're a believer, God is calling you to join Him. Your response is to say "Here am I, Lord. Send me." Don't you want to get in on the blessing and bring the kindness, justice, and righteousness of the kingdom of heaven into your world like a true child of God?

Does that seem like a tall order? You can do it because God has equipped you and prepared you.

Trust Christ (your Prince of Peace) and receive peace with God, the forgiveness of sins, and eternal life.

Connect in a group where you can love and be loved by others.

Serve in ministry beyond yourself at church.

Give, trusting God with your tithe and offerings. A missions offering is about peacemaking in the world, contributing to your eternal investment portfolio.

Pray and go. Find your edge and enter the mission field for a short term or long term.

Where's your edge? I went over the edge, rappelling a ten-story building. Jesus went over the edge for you, from heaven to a cross, into a grave and then rising again. You don't have to go to India or Africa to find your edge, but wherever God is calling you, that's where you should go.

Where can you make peace right now? Where could you follow Christ on mission? You might want to say, "I'm not sure I'm able." Listen, it's not your *ability* but your *availability* God is seeking. Maybe you can say, "I'm not there yet, but I'm open. What can I do?" Start choosing the way of peace. Ask God where in your decisions, your heart, and your home you can promote the way of peace.

Making peace and facing pressure are part of the blessing in Kingdom Adventure. Those who join God in this work welcome heaven to earth.

Where's your edge? What is God calling you to be and do?

How might God use you to make a difference in the lives of others?

What is God saying to you through this chapter?

CHAPTER 24

THE COST OF FOLLOWING JESUS

"Blessed are those who are persecuted because of righteousness, for theirs is the kingdom of heaven."

I take up my cross.

In his book *Holy Sweat,* Tim Hansel quotes Lois Chaney regarding the high cost of loving people:

> He saw people love each other . . . and he saw that all love made strenuous demands on the lovers. He saw love requires sacrifice and self-denial. He saw love produce arguments and anguish . . . and he decided that it cost too much. And he decided not to diminish his life with love.
>
> He saw people strive for distant and hazy goals. He saw men strive for success . . . women strive for high, high, ideals . . . and he saw that the striving was frequently mixed with disappointment and he saw the strong men fail . . . he saw it force people into pettiness . . . he saw that those who succeeded were sometimes those who

had not earned the success. And he decided that it cost too much. He decided not to soil his life with striving.

He saw people serving others. He saw men give money to the poor and helpless . . . and he saw that the more they served, the faster the need grew . . . he saw ungrateful receivers turn on their serving friends . . . he decided not to soil his life with serving.

And when he died, he walked up to God and presented him with his life. Undiminished, unmarred, and unsoiled. His life was clean from the filth of the world, and he presented it proudly . . . saying, "This is my life," and the great God said, "What life?"[11]

We come to the final beatitudes with perhaps Jesus' most alarming blessings. Twice, Jesus says that blessings come through persecution. How do you think that landed on the ears of His original hearers? Imagine a conversation between some people listening that day and Jesus:

"Wait a minute, let me get this straight. We're on the high-end side of spiritual maturity now, right?"

"Right."

"Deep transformation is taking place, and we've joined the ranks of the peacemakers, those who're taking the initiative to share the message of redemption with the world, the ones who are bearing the likeness of Christ and are called children of God, right?"

"Right."

"We've been credited with the righteousness of Christ, so we're now devoted to living righteous lives for right reasons. We're on the solution side of the equation, right?"

"Right."

"We're joining God in His work to share the peace of Christ with others, right?"

"Right."

"We're sowing the seed of God's truth and harvesting its fruit in other's lives, right?"

"Right."

"And now you're saying the next level of blessing in store for us is persecution?"

"That's right, the blessing of persecution. If you follow Me with all your heart, you will be misunderstood, misrepresented, mistreated, insulted, gossiped about, maligned, ridiculed, and persecuted. But when you see these things happening, don't be alarmed. Instead, throw a party! Do a happy dance! Why? Two reasons. First, your reward in heaven is great. And second, you're being treated the way God's change agents are always treated. You're in the company of the prophets."

Jesus isn't glamorizing martyrdom. Human life is precious, and every person is an image bearer of almighty God. Every life matters so much to God that Christ suffered the agony and shame of a Roman executioner's rack to love and redeem every one of us as if there were only one of us. By the same token, neither is He making a merely hypothetical point. It costs to follow Jesus in this world.

Estimates are that more Christians were martyred for their faith in the twentieth century than in all previous centuries combined.[12] One report claims that 400 Christians are killed each day worldwide right now. That's one every four minutes.[13] Paul told Timothy, "Everyone who wants to live a godly life in Christ Jesus will be persecuted" (2 Timothy 3:12). Jesus told His disciples in the Upper Room before He was crucified, "'A servant is not greater than his master.' If they persecuted me, they will persecute you also" (John 15:20).

If the Christian life is a bed of roses, then it comes complete with thorns—a crown of thorns. In spite of what some modern preachers promise, God hasn't assured His followers of a problem-free life. In fact, following Jesus inevitably *invites* trouble. Here's the promise: if you get involved in Jesus' story, trouble is going to find you.

In virtually every field of study or work, when people stand up for Jesus, someone tries to knock them down. We need to understand this fact, anticipate it, and be ready for it. Persecution, in any of its forms, isn't an aberration in the Christian life; it's part of the normal Christian life. Let me be clear: if we're being persecuted for being obnoxious, God certainly won't bless us. But if we're ridiculed and abused for expressing the truth in love, just like Jesus did, we'll receive a prophet's blessing.

In this beatitude, you begin to understand what Paul meant when he tells the Philippians about sharing the "fellowship of [Jesus'] sufferings" (Philippians 3:10 KJV); when he tells the Corinthians, "We always carry around in our body the death of Jesus, so that the life of Jesus may also be revealed in our body" (2 Corinthians 4:10); and when he tells the Romans, "We face death all day long" (Romans 8:36). This is what Jesus was talking about when He told His disciples, "Whoever wants to be my disciple must deny themselves and take up their cross daily and follow me. For whoever wants to save their life will lose it, but whoever loses their life for me will save it" (Luke 9:23-24).

When you join God in His work in the field that's white with harvest, it doesn't take long to discover it's also a battlefield where we fight an enemy who isn't eager to lose or release anyone held captive. And suddenly, you're in the target zone. Why? Because you've become dangerous—a threat to the evil one. God is using you to set captives free, to help others break the shackles of evil through the gospel of Christ, and to slice through the deceit of spiritual darkness and help them come into the life, love, and light of Christ. And they are coming the same way you did, by admitting their need, feeling and grieving their lack to the point they are willing to yield their will to God and receive His salvation. God is using you to invade the enemy's territory and help others find freedom in Jesus. That makes you dangerous, a threat to the spiritual enemy.

Are you ready for the fight?

Did you sign up to be persecuted for your stand for Christ? Explain your answer.

Why is it crucial to realize that suffering is a normal part of the Christian life?

What is God saying to you through this chapter?

CHAPTER 25

ARE YOU A THREAT?

In Acts 19, Luke tells the story of how God's power was so strong in Paul that extraordinary miracles were happening through him: sick bodies were healed and evil spirits expelled. Some spiritualist on-lookers were so impressed that they thought they would give it a try. They went around saying to those who were demon possessed, "In the name of Jesus, whom Paul preaches, I command you to come out." And one day an evil spirit answered them: "Jesus I know, and Paul I know about, but who are you?" Then he jumped on them and beat them up until "they ran out of the house naked and bleeding" (Acts 19:11-16).

Notice that the bad guy in the story, the evil spirit, had some knowledge. What was known? He knew Jesus. He knew Paul. He knew the imposters were frauds and hypocrites. He also knew the posers were spiritual cream puffs. He knew Jesus and Paul were armed and dangerous, thoroughly equipped to do damage to the stronghold of evil.

As a parent, I can tell you I was always pleased when my children's names showed up on the Dean's List. I was thrilled for them to be on the honor roll for outstanding performance at school. It's one thing to show up on the Dean's List, but it takes honor to an entirely new level to have your name show up on the Devil's List. I don't know about you, but I want the demons to know my name. "Jesus I know. Paul I know. Bill? Oh yes, I know him!" That has a nice sound to my ears. Does the devil know your name?

Why does persecution come to those who live godly lives? First, we are living in enemy-occupied territory with values that are diametrically opposed to God's rule. In this fallen world system, Jesus said that we will have tribulation (John 16:33). Think of yourself in a stream with a swift current. That's our culture that values beauty, brains, and brawn—to the point of idolatry. In Christ, you have now turned upstream against the current and are swimming headfirst into the flow. The current is the pressure for you to "go along to get along," and peer pressure tries to force you into compliance. The fact that you refuse to succumb to the pressure creates turbulence.

Second, as Christ lives in you and your life reflects more of His glory, you become a threat to the bad guys. In John's first letter, he reminds us, "The one who is in you is greater than the one who is in the world" (1 John 4:4). You become a threat to the world's values because you know, love, and follow Jesus, and you reflect the glory of the true and living God. But that's not all: You're a threat to religious traditionalism and legalistic moralism because you are alive in true holiness by grace. God's life bursts through the dry wineskins of humanistic religion with the fresh, new wine of the Spirit—and this new wine needs new wineskins of a loving, compassionate, godly life. But don't be surprised if the legalists accuse you of being soft on sin or that you've compromised the gospel because your mission has you keeping company with sinners. Didn't the legalists of Jesus' day malign Him in the same way when they accused Him of being a "friend of sinners"?

On the other hand, you become a threat to blatant sinfulness and immoral relativism because the light of Christ's truth is shining in and through your life and dispelling the darkness. You're not being held captive by the same sin that holds others prisoner. So, don't be surprised if secularists think you're too strict and narrow minded. They may even call you a bigot. To them you're just not "fun" anymore.

But you know you aren't soft on sin. In fact, you hate it. You fear it. You know how deceptive and destructive it is. But neither are you a bigot. You truly love people. You love them to the point that you don't want to see any of them lost. You know in your heart of hearts that you're not compromising, but you aren't judgmental either. The things being said about you simply aren't true, so why are people ridiculing you? For Jesus' sake. You're walking with Him. You're standing in the same gap where He made intercession for Pharisees and prostitutes alike—at the cross. And He's using you as an instrument of His grace and truth to help set the captives free. That's why we're threats to the enemy . . . and to the people who are, at least for now, allied with the enemy.

How can we be a threat to the enemy without being obnoxious to people who are in the enemy's camp?

How did Jesus treat people who opposed Him? How can you follow His example?

What is God saying to you through this chapter?

CHAPTER 26

PERSECUTION PRINCIPLES

What are we to do with the conflicts we face? We need to do three simple but crucial things:

First, expect conflict. As we've seen, criticism and misrepresentation are part of the package of true spiritual growth and kingdom blessings. Let this sink in: "Blessed are the persecuted." Don't be crushed by criticism; be encouraged. A moving ship always makes waves. Tall trees catch a lot of wind. Newton's third law of motion is: "For every action, there is an equal and opposite reaction." But you may have never heard of Harrison's Postulate: "For every action, there is an equal and opposite *criticism*."[14] Dale Carnegie said, "Any fool can criticize, condemn, and complain . . . and most of them do." Billy Graham knew criticism all of his life. In 1993 a fundamentalist Christian leader said Graham "has done more to harm the cause of Christ than any other living man."[15] If he experienced unjust criticism, we will too. We need to state the obvious: If nobody's criticizing you, it may mean you're not doing anything worth noticing. But if you're going to be criticized, it might as well be for doing something!

Second, let the conflict push you toward your kingdom inheritance. When pressure comes, don't let it push you away from heaven. Let it push you closer to it. This world isn't all there is. Jesus said there are *rewards* coming in heaven. Just because we don't make headlines down here doesn't mean we aren't front page news in heaven. Jesus said there's joy in heaven every time a sinner repents (Luke 15:10). Think higher. Aim higher. "Set your minds on things above" (Colossians 3:2). As you join God in His redemptive purpose, you'll also join Him in great reward.

And third, be happy as you find your voice among the change agents of God. You and I can't begin to imagine how God envisions us. He sees our names listed right up there with Isaiah, Jeremiah, Amos, Hosea, and Elijah. He sees all of His children keeping company with His prophets—the ones who saved their lives by losing them for God. He envisions your life, for its brief time on earth, impacting eternity as you obey His call and do His will.

Let God use persecution as fertilizer to help you grow. Now that you've got everybody's attention, seize the day and make it a teachable moment. E. Stanley Jones wrote, "Self-surrender is the greatest emancipation that ever comes to a human being. Seek first the kingdom of God and all things will be added to you—including yourself."[16]

Jesus said. "Whoever loses their life for me will save it" (Matthew 16:25). Do you want to find yourself, truly? . . . deeply? . . . eternally? Then be courageous and take up your cross. Follow Jesus wherever He leads and let yourself become a target of the enemy. Jesus told us to "deny" ourselves. That doesn't mean we lose our identity or personality. He was talking about saying "no" to our inherent selfishness and saying "yes" to following Him. As we follow, He will show the forgiven man how to be a forgiving man. He will teach the healed woman how to become a healing woman. He'll use those of us who have been rescued from sin, death, and hell to rescue others with the gospel of grace.

The writer to the Hebrews gives us a clear picture of the source of our courage. He tells us to fix our eyes on Jesus, "the author and finisher of our faith; who for the joy that was set before him endured the cross, despising the shame, and is set down at the right hand of the throne of God" (Hebrews 12:2 KJV).

The day will come when we'll sit down with Jesus, but the day of celebration and parades doesn't come until *after* the battle has been won. If we "fix our eyes" on those who oppose us, we'll either become furious or we'll be cowards. If we "fix our eyes" on the hurt they inflict, we'll become bitter and full of self-pity. But if we "fix our eyes" on the One who endured incredible hostility for our sake, we'll stay strong, and we'll make a difference. God "gives us the victory through our Lord Jesus Christ" (1 Corinthians 15:57). Now is the time for us to get in the game, to fight the good fight, to grow in grace, to yield our lives fully and follow Jesus. That's the Kingdom Adventure.

How would you describe our "kingdom inheritance"?

What are some ways persecution deepens our faith and tenderizes our hearts?

What is God saying to you through this chapter?

KINGDOM AUDACITY

"Blessed are you when people insult you, persecute you and falsely say all kinds of evil against you because of me. Rejoice and be glad, because great is your reward in heaven, for in the same way they persecuted the prophets who were before you."

(Matthew 5:11-12)

CHAPTER 27

LIVING LARGE

"Blessed are you when people insult you, persecute you and falsely say all kinds of evil against you because of me. Rejoice and be glad, because great is your reward in heaven, for in the same way they persecuted the prophets who were before you."

I impact eternity.

Have you ever done anything really *audacious*? Audacity is a noun. It means "a willingness to take surprisingly bold risks." On the negative side, it can mean "rudeness or disrespect." On the positive, it means "daring or grit."

When I think back over the course of my life, the most audacious thing that comes to my mind was proposing to Lisa . . . over the phone. Yes, I did that. It was a black rotary dial telephone. I assure you, I wasn't trying to live by the definition of audacity. I had an "aha" moment and felt the most honorable thing I could do with it was tell Lisa the truth. Let me explain.

We'd been away from each other for quite a while, literally in different states. That was long before the days of Facetime or Skype. When we last parted, neither of us knew where the relationship was going. I went to Oklahoma to be a student pastor, and she stayed in

Missouri in ministry. One afternoon I was looking at her picture and started to write her a letter. In no time, it was twelve handwritten pages, and by the end of it, I wrote, "I guess what I'm trying to say is, I love you."

The words on the page were surprising to me. Some guys are free with those words in relationships with women, but not me. I told myself that if I *ever* told a woman "I love you," another question should immediately follow, and that was precisely my dilemma. I was sitting there looking at her picture and what I'd written, and I wrote the follow up question: "I guess what I really mean is, Will you be my wife?" I stared at the letter, and I told myself, *I can't put this in the mail! I gotta call her.* And I did.

When she answered the phone, she was a bit surprised to hear from me since we'd left things open-ended when we'd said goodbye. I said, "Lisa, I was just writing you a letter and wondered if I could I read it to you?"

She said, "Yes."

So I read it. When I finished, it was quiet on the other end. Really quiet.

Finally, Lisa asked, "Do you want my answer now?"

I mumbled, "Well, I want you to know where I stand."

She told me, "Well, I want to be your wife."

I was shocked. I stammered, "You do?!"

And so it began. The *audacity*! And yet can I tell you? The blessing!

When have you taken a risk, shown some courage, followed your heart, and pushed through your fear? Maybe others didn't (and still don't) understand why you took that bold step, and maybe you don't either, but a door opened and a blessing came—the blessing of audacity.

The final beatitude is your personal pathway to the blessing of Kingdom Audacity. However, this one, even more than the others, probably isn't going to make sense. You may never have tried it or seen it work. Let me give you a word of warning: This message isn't "chef Jesus" sending leftovers home from feeding the thousands. No, this beatitude is "disciple-maker Jesus" developing leaders for high impact. If you're looking for a snack pack of spiritual treats, they won't be on the menu. This is Jesus, the audacious.

If there ever was a blessing in disguise, this is it. This is when the persecution gets personal. You're doing what God has led you to do, the best you know how, and it has taken you into a thornbush of ridicule and rejection. You're experiencing a buzz saw ravaging your reputation with slander, gossip, and character assassination. You thought you were just following Jesus and look what happened!

And here's the most audacious part. Jesus says when *that* happens, rejoice! And not just with your voice: the literal meaning of *be glad* is put your body into it and *jump for* joy. That's *audacity*!

No, you're thinking, *that's insanity.* What if I told you Jesus is teaching His followers to practice spiritual judo, the kind to use when you find yourself in such personal disagreement with others that they attack you, put you down, make fun of you, blackball you, and worse. And they may not know it, but all you're really trying to do is follow Christ. In judo, you use your opponent's strengths against him, but this requires insight and experience. When you're ridiculed, you're tempted to give up on the whole enterprise, go your own way, lash back, fight fire with fire, act ugly, and let fear drive you to be angry and defensive. For many, maybe you, this will be your *least* favorite beatitude because it's the one *most* contrary to your egocentric life that values popularity and prestige above all else. I don't mean to offend you. I assure you that I speak from personal experience. If you've ever prayed, "God, please free me from myself," here's the way He answers this prayer. In a world where we are commercialized to be full of ourselves, this is completely contrarian.

I had two favorite cakes as a kid growing up: angel food, all fluffy and big, and pineapple upside-down cake, gooey and warm. Both of them are served *downside up*. In this beatitude, Jesus shows us how to turn *downside up* in life. The downside of life is typically accompanied by fear—fear of pain, fear of loss, fear of the unknown that might happen. I think Jesus is teaching His followers how to overcome fear. Fear isn't always bad: fear of man is a snare, but the fear of the Lord is secret wisdom. This lesson is precisely what some spiritual warriors need right now.

You weren't looking for a fight. You're just trying to follow Jesus, and *bam!* The weapons of the evil one, the weapons of the world, are to shame, blame, and defame. Jesus says, "Yes, but you can squeeze blessing out of that. When people *insult* you, *revile* you, show their teeth to disgrace and discredit you . . . when they *persecute*—hunt you to trap or overtake . . . when they *falsely say evil*, using wicked, malicious lies with intention to deceive, mislead, and hurt . . . when they do such things *because of Me*, don't give up or give in! Keep trusting. Keep fighting. And keep believing that I'm using all this for good."

What can you do? Practice your judo moves. Use the persecution to make you stronger and wiser. Be audacious. Instead of crumbling in fear or exploding in anger, let the joy of the Lord be your strength.

Did you know this is the first beatitude that gives you a present active imperative verb? A challenge to *do* something? What is it? *Rejoice*—lean consciously toward joy and delight in grace. Rejoicing isn't a feeling; it's a choice to be glad and jump for joy in the present. Why? Because something wonderful is coming in the future (great is your reward in heaven) and something connects you to the past (this is how the prophets were treated). Now, you're counted with them. Imagine that: *you* are numbered with the prophets, God's remarkable change agents.

Does this sound impossible? You may assume you're like the caterpillar who saw a butterfly and said, "You'll never get me up in one of those!" I understand. You're not a prophet and didn't ask to be one. But here's Jesus' bottom line: You can live larger than the hurt; you can live for God. Press through your fear with joy the way the prophets did. How do you behave like a prophet? Here's how: keep your eyes on God, humble your heart in obedience, keep the main thing the main thing, and take joy in your greater God. This statement helps me keep the right perspective:

> Show greater faith in your Greater God
> to do a greater thing.

As you follow Christ, you're going to find yourself in disagreements with others, and sometimes you'll face genuine hostility. Jesus says, "Don't be daunted by the disruption." There's blessing even there. But the blessing doesn't come in vilifying or demonizing your opponent. We don't get the reward by lashing back but in responding with confidence in a larger reality: God is bigger than your smear and bigger than your fear. *Rejoice* in His bigness.

Live larger than the disagreement: "Disagree without dishonoring." Don't be surprised when you have disagreements with all kinds of people about all kinds of things, but in them, treat people the way Jesus did, with the beautiful blend of grace and truth.

Are you naturally a risk-taker or are you risk-averse? How can you follow Jesus in this beatitude?

What do you think is the promised reward for faith-empowred audacity?

What is God saying to you through this chapter?

CHAPTER 28

LOVE THEM ANYWAY

Sometimes, we fight to the death over issues that aren't of supreme importance. One way to show greater faith in our greater God is to understand there are negotiables and non-negotiables. A grid many believers have used for centuries identifies three parts of a paradigm. The concept helps us disagree while still honoring one another. Three levels are: absolutes, convictions, and preferences.

Let me describe the distinctions: absolutes are truths that are *absolutely essential for* salvation in Christ; convictions are truths distinctive to your biblical interpretation; and preferences are opinions, which are judgments we make because of personal and cultural familiarity.

Absolutes include the deity of Christ, His death in our place, His bodily resurrection and return, salvation by grace through faith, and a commitment to follow the Great Commandment and Great Commission. These are essentials in following Christ.

Convictions aren't essential to salvation, and they are concepts Christians differ on. Convictions are Bible teachings distinctive to your faith tradition, like predestination and free will, how we understand sanctification and holiness, the mode of baptism, the meaning of communion, charismatic gifts, some moral issues, and politics. Christians can disagree on these (as maybe you've noticed) but still agree they aren't essential to eternal salvation.

Preferences are choices we practice because of cultural familiarity, such as a preferred dress codes for church, music styles, tattoos, movies we watch, and so on. Christians get ourselves in trouble when we elevate a preference or conviction as if it was an absolute . . . and reject anyone who disagrees. Jesus never did that.

Paul addresses the issue using two words in Roman 14:1: "disputable matters." He means that arguments can be made on all sides of convictions and preferences. He says, "Accept the one whose faith is weak, without quarreling over disputable matters." It's possible to disagree without harshly judging others.

In fact, Christ-followers are to behave as Christ did—in love. Paul was very clear: "Love is the fulfillment of the law" (Roman 13:10; Galatians 5:14; James 2:8). And as we've seen, Jesus gives us a high benchmark: "By this everyone will know that you are my disciples, if you love one another" (John 13:35). Augustine has been credited with saying, "In essentials unity, in nonessentials liberty, in all things charity."

Some battles aren't worth fighting. Fight with a skunk and you may win, but you won't smell the same. And you certainly don't have to put the skunk in your trunk and drive it around with you wherever you go! When others provoke you and try to prevent you from doing God's will, Jesus says for us to respond with joy and squeeze the blessing out of the insult.

A poem by Edwin Markham about the inclusive power of love tells us:

> He drew a circle that left me out;
> Heretic, rebel, a thing to flout.
> But love and I had the wit to win;
> We drew a circle that drew him in.[17]

The audacity! Have you heard the hymn "There's a Wideness in God's Mercy"?

> But we make His love too narrow
> by false limits of our own
> and we magnify His strictness
> with a zeal he will not own.
> For the love of God is broader
> than the measure of the mind;
> and the heart of the Eternal
> is most wonderfully kind.[18]

I've long had this practice for dealing with critics: I listen, I learn, I love. "Love never fails." I let critics say whatever they want to say, I learn from the best leaders, and then I lead my life way I believe God wants me to.

To the directive to listen, learn, and love, Jesus would add, "Laugh!" Choose joy in the Lord. (I've seen the T-shirt that reads: "Live, Love, Learn, Laugh." We should all get one and wear it.) Rejoice and jump for joy, especially when the heat is on. Jesus' half-brother James gave this directive: "Consider it pure joy, my brothers and sisters, whenever you face trials of many kinds, because you know that the testing of your faith produces perseverance. Let perseverance finish its work so that you may be mature and complete, not lacking anything" (James 1:2-4). I believe he's saying, "When people condemn you unfairly, show greater faith in your greater God to do a greater thing."

God is bigger than your fear, the intimidating critic, the injustice, the unfairness, the not-rightness, the humiliation, and the manipulation of it all. Find your joy in Jesus and live larger than the conflict. Rejoice in the rewards that are coming in heaven and the fact that you're numbered with the prophets.

I read of some mountain climbers ascending the Matterhorn in the Swiss Alps. Two were experienced guides, and the third was making his first climb. When they reached the top, the veterans moved aside to let the new climber have the first look. As he went up the summit and was about to stand, his guides pulled him down. He blurted out, "What are you doing?"

One of the guides told him, "Hold up your hand."

He did and felt the full force of the wind.

The guide explained, "Up here, the only safe place is on your knees."

This is the summit of the Beatitudes; the high point of maturity in Christ—and the only safe place—is on your knees.

The first people to hear Jesus teach this downside-up principle were under a corrupt king and an oppressive government. Persecution was very real. They probably wanted to shout, "What blessing are you talking about, Jesus?" Maybe you want to shout too? I don't blame you—it sounds more like a curse than a blessing. But Jesus is saying, "Even when facing the curses of a fallen world, don't fear. Let God flip it."

Maturity in the Christian life is downside up and upside down— realizing that a blessed life includes personally identifying with the suffering of Christ. Our culture is full of pain avoiders, and many are addicted to painkillers. But Jesus says, "Let God meet you in the pain and take you higher."

Christ knows things in the kingdom that we don't know. He shows it on the cross when He says "Father forgive them. They don't know what they're doing." Christ has the audacity to *love* his persecutors.

What does love do? It casts out fear. It never fails. That's the larger blessing.

We're called to unleash the power of love. If anything is worth being persecuted for, that's it. You may be called names for following Jesus, and you may be misunderstood and mistreated, but you have the power of choice. You can make the choice to change your point of view and your point of reference, and then rejoice in the middle of the persecution. You can trust Jesus and persevere through the pain. Don't give up too soon. The game's not done until sudden death overtime . . . and in the end, we always win.

What happens when we fight over the wrong things? Do you need to make any adjustments in what you argue about? Explain your answer.

How can we truly love those who disagree with us?

What is God saying to you through this chapter?

CHAPTER 29

NEXT STEPS

In these chapters on the Beatitudes, we've looked at the four levels of impact, we've seen the Hero, and we've dug deep into each of the nine crucial promises of blessing. We began with Kingdom Access, which includes a gate with three hinges: we recognize that we're poor in spirit (I admit my need); we mourn our condition (I grieve my lack); and we become meek and trusting (I yield my will). These form the open door to life in the Spirit.

We explored the truths of Kingdom Affluence. We hunger and thirst for God's righteousness to be credited to our account (I experience God's life); we become channels of God's mercy (I share God's love); and we trust God to purify our motives, our desires, and our behavior (I see God's light).

The third level of impact is Kingdom Adventure. Jesus came to offer peace with God through His death and resurrection, and we have the honor of being His hands, feet, and voice in a world desperately in need of His grace (I join God's work). As we go to tell people about Jesus, we can expect to be treated with the same contempt people had (and still have) for Him (I take up my cross).

And finally, we saw that a grasp of God's grace produces Kingdom Audacity in us. We, like the prophets before us, endure persecution and the lies of those who oppose us. But as we remain faithful, God uses us to share the message of hope in the gospel of grace, and He gives us the privilege of helping others take steps along the spiritual growth continuum, so they, too, have an impact on the world (I impact eternity).

What does it take to have this kind of impact on the people around us? I believe we need both tenderness and tenacity, grace and truth, humility and courage. These pairs of traits temper each other, deepen each other, and put us in touch with the heart of Jesus.

We can be sure that the enemy of our souls will fight us every step of the way. C.S. Lewis observed that Christians usually make one of two mistakes in dealing with Satan: we give him too much credit or not enough credit; we're obsessed with him or we totally ignore him. The devil is very real, but his power is limited. His ploys are deception (lies about the nature of God, His forgiveness, and His purpose for us), temptation (to make secondary things more attractive than primary things), and accusation (whispering or shouting that our sins are too great to be forgiven and that we're utter failures). In our battle with the forces of darkness, we have God's truth to point us to Him and instruct us to trust Him in the most difficult situations; we have the Spirit of God to guide, comfort, and empower us; and we have the family of God to encourage and support us.

It's our privilege and responsibility to leave a legacy to the people around us, and especially, to the next generation. Our task isn't only to apply the four levels of impact in our own lives, but to "pay it forward" to the people in our groups, the people in our families, the people in our churches, and the people in our communities. Be a channel, not a bottle.

When Jesus listed the Beatitudes in His famous sermon, He was just getting started. Immediately after this section of His sermon, Jesus uses two metaphors to describe the kind of influence we have as we experience the blessings of the Beatitudes: salt and light. As we near the end of this study, remember that God has made you salt to add flavor to your interactions and make people thirsty for Jesus, and

He has made you light to illuminate His grace and truth for everyone to see. Jesus tells us:

> "You are the salt of the earth. But if the salt loses its saltiness, how can it be made salty again? It is no longer good for anything, except to be thrown out and trampled underfoot.
>
> You are the light of the world. A town built on a hill cannot be hidden. Neither do people light a lamp and put it under a bowl. Instead they put it on its stand, and it gives light to everyone in the house. In the same way, let your light shine before others, that they may see your good deeds and glorify your Father in heaven." (Matthew 5:13-16)

Never forget who you are, how much you're loved, and the high calling to represent your King.

What kind of legacy do you want to leave?

What are the properties of salt and light? What does it look like for us to live out these characteristics?

What is God saying to you through this chapter?

CHAPTER 30

FROM "KNOW HOW" TO "SHOW HOW"

It's no surprise that we live in a time of urgency. At Christ Journey, we often remind each other:

People are dying,
Lives are in the balance,
Families are on the brink,
Eternity is at stake.

It's not unusual in our world to hear people whine and moan about "how bad things are," wondering—even despairing—about the future. They experience harm, but they don't have hope. The Jesus I know feels our pain, can relate to the trouble we're in, and understands the deep needs of our world. It's for this purpose He came. I believe it's for this purpose He gave us the Beatitudes—as our pathway to blessing, even in the midst of circumstances we would never normally consider blessings.

But here's how God surprises us: His goal, His purpose, the intended outcome of God's engaging us in His "upside-down kingdom" is that He might use us as instruments of His grace and peace in the midst of the upside-downness of the world. As we grow through the journey of faith, propelled by the transformational process we encounter in the Beatitudes, we emerge on the other end as influencers in the redemption and growth of others.

Surprise! *You* are the light of the world, placed in it to outshine the darkness. *You* are the salt of the earth, filled with the qualities that can fight spiritual dry rot and moral decay . . . not merely by the power of rules enforced by law but by the power of a loving, wise, strong character that has an impact as it makes contact with a world in need.

Jesus used another metaphor that illustrates this same truth. In Matthew 13:33 He says, "The kingdom of heaven is like yeast that a woman took and mixed into [a large amount] of flour until it worked all through the dough." Jesus envisions His followers to be instruments of blessing, ambassadors of God's dynamic life "working all through the dough" wherever we find ourselves in our culture. From the marketplace, where we spend from sixty to seventy-five percent of our waking hours as adults, to the mission field where we respond to the needs of the orphan, the poor, the oppressed, neglected, and abused.

It's not enough for the Christ-follower to be personally blessed and transformed by the redeeming grace and truth of God. God's desire is that each of us now turn *know how* into *show how*. We are to live our lives as spillways of blessing so others not only get in the *flow* but also get in the *grow* for themselves, so they can now become part of the transforming river of Spirit life God is unleashing to water our world.

Paul affirms this divine expectation as he writes to Timothy, "You then, my son, be strong in the grace that is in Christ Jesus. And the things you have heard me say in the presence of many witnesses entrust to reliable people who will also be qualified to teach others" (2 Timothy 2:1-2). First, Paul challenges Timothy to stay connected to the strength God provides by His grace in Christ—just as Jesus encourages His listeners to be salt that keeps its flavor and light that isn't dimmed by being covered. Then, Paul tells Timothy to turn his *know how* into *show how* to help others find their way into the fullness of God by modeling, mentoring, and multiplying divine influence through others on the journey. Jesus wants us to multiply our impact in the same way.

If you have now learned how to live in the path of blessing by journeying with Jesus through the upside-down kingdom in the Beatitudes, it's your turn to pass it on by showing someone else how to do it. Ask God who He would have you engage on the journey, someone you could help raise up who would then, in turn, raise up others. One of my mentors taught me to look for "FAT Hungry" disciples—people who are Faithful, Available, Teachable, and Hungry for God! These are the ones God will use to change the world.

At this writing it has been my privilege to teach these concepts to hungry leaders in Rwanda, India, Cuba, Lebanon, and Brazil, as well as the United States. As you hear the call of God to this most noble and worthy task, may He grace you to respond as Isaiah did: "Here am I, Lord. Send me!"

Where are you in the process of turning your "know how" to "show how"?

Who are you pouring your life into? (Or who is on your short list?) What difference will it make in their lives? . . . and yours?

What is God saying to you through this chapter?

ENDNOTES

1   Cited in *American Cowboy*, September-October 1997, p. 79.

2   Dallas Willard, *The Divine Conspiracy* (New York: Harper, 1998), p. 100.

3   Ibid., pp. 123-124.

4   hollywood.com, Jul. 9, 2003

5   Carl F. Henry, *Baker's Dictionary of Christian Ethics* (Grand Rapids: Baker Book House, 1973), p. 418.

6   William Shakespeare, *The Merchant of Venice*, Act IV, Scene I.

7   Cited by Justin Phillips in *C.S. Lewis in a Time of War: The World War II Broadcasts* (Grand Rapids: Zondervan, 2006), p. 167.

8   Frederick Dale Bruner, *Matthew: A Commentary Vol. 1* (Grand Rapids: Eerdmans Publishing, 2007), p. 146.

9   From "It Is Well with My Soul" by Horatio Spafford, 1873.

10   Steven Curtis Chapman, "The Great Adventure," lyrics by Steven Curtis Chapman and Geoff Moore, Capitol Music Group

11   Cited in *The Me God Sees* by Roberta Kuhne.

12   Philip Graham Ryken, *My Father's World* (Presbyterian and Reformed Publishing Company, 2002), p 29.

13 Raymond McHenry, *McHenry's Stories for the Soul* (Hendrickson Publishing, 2002).

14 *The Rotarian*, August 1994, p. 56.

15 McHenry, *Stories*, p. 64.

16 E. Stanley Jones, *The Unshakable Kingdom and the Unchanging Person* (CreateSpace, 2017), p. 102.

17 "Outwitted," Edwin Markham (1852-1940), cited in the *Harvard Business Review*, 2011, p. 108.

18 "There's a Wideness in God's Mercy," lyrics by Frederick W. Faber (1814-1863).

ACKNOWLEDGMENTS

This book has been under construction for years, and I'm indebted to so many for so much.

Thank you to the outstanding staff and pastors of Christ Journey who have carried the load to give me time to write, and also, have lived and applied these truths in their own lives and ministry.

Thank you to the amazing Christ Journey Church family who are right now traveling the pathway to blessing and using it as a tool for transformational living, believing "as God made room for us, we are now privileged to make room for others."

Thank you to the mentors who helped me learn how to let my life come alive through God's Word by entering the story and helping others do the same: Pastor Ken Dodson, Leila Wilson, Dr. Boo Heflin, Bertha Smith, and Pastor Dan Yeary.

My heartfelt gratitude to each one of the people who reviewed this book and offered their kind words of support and endorsement. Your generous and thoughtful encouragement is a tremendous blessing.

Thank you to Steve Blount and Pat Springle for helping bring it to publication. Thank you Vannia Enriquez and Yukiko Centeno for your amazing cover photo and design.

Thank you to my parents, LaVeta and William L., whose faith adventure led them "Go west" from Missouri, obeying God's call to volunteer to serve the Native American peoples of Arizona. Thank you for going, not knowing what awaited you on and off the reservation.

Thank you to Lisa, my wife, and Corrie and Jess, my daughters, who for years have listened repeatedly as the ideas for this book were born, lived, and given shape in the real-life crucibles of our home and church. I love you.

ABOUT THE AUTHOR

Bill White is the long time Senior Pastor of Christ Journey Church in Miami, Florida. The multi-thousand-member church currently has three campuses and is launching a fourth on Miami Beach spring of 2020. Its members come from over 50 nations and speak 29 languages. According to Google analytics Christ Journey Church Online's reach has totaled 186,598 unique users from 198 countries and territories. Journey Church annually initiates a collection and distribution of goods through its FeedMiami emphasis that serves the food insecure of our area, including families at risk, single moms, and former victims of domestic violence and human trafficking. Eighteen tons were given away this past year to feed 9700 people.

His community service includes multiple roles with Baptist Health South Florida where he was past Chairman of the Board of Trustees. He also serves on the boards of Baptist Hospital of Miami and the Miami Cancer Institute and is Board Chairman with Agape Ministry for women and children. He regularly teaches at MiamiLead in Coral Gables and has taught spiritual life and leadership principles internationally including Rwanda, Lebanon, Brazil, India, and Cuba.

Pastor Bill holds three earned degrees: a BA from William Jewell College, and the Master of Divinity and Doctor of Ministry degrees from Southwestern Baptist Theological Seminary. Additionally he has done post-graduate studies at Baylor University and the University of Virginia.

He and Lisa have two grown daughters and two brilliant grandsons. His adventures have taken him free diving in the Bahamas, rappelling a waterfall in North Carolina, mountain biking and hang gliding in the Tetons, skydiving with the Golden Knights and riding his Harley and several horses as audacious opportunity presents. So far he has only broken ten different bones.

RESOURCES

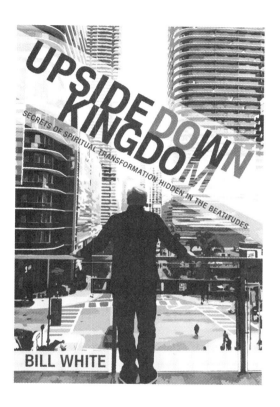

To order additional copies of this book go to
pastorbillwhite.com

The eBook is available at Amazon.com

An audiobook plus Spanish print and eBook versions
are coming in 2020.